Robert Frost in Russia

Robert Frost in Russia

F.D. Reeve

ZEPHYR PRESS

This reissue of *Robert Frost in Russia* would not have been possible without the active cooperation and support of many people, beginning with some of the principals in the story, most particularly Jack Matlock and Stewart Udall. Further assistance came from Dorothy Call Catherman, Peter Davison, Ellen Elias-Bursac, John McCarthy, Ina Nenortas, Leonid Pevzner, Mimi Ross, Tom Tuck, and Thomas Venclova.

Zephyr Press acknowledges with further gratitude the financial support of the Tiny Tiger Foundation, Charles Merrill, and the Massachusetts Cultural Council.

MASSACHUSETTS CULTURAL COUNCIL

for William Meredith

> *That was what he wanted to hear,*
> *Something you had done too exactly for words,*
> *Maybe, but too exactly to lie about either.*

Over My Shoulder

On March 26, 1959, Frost's publishers gave him an eighty-fifth birthday dinner in the Waldorf-Astoria. Lionel Trilling astounded the literary world by calling Frost on "his massive, his Sophoclean birthday,…a terrifying poet," who, like the other great writers of the classic American tradition, radically sloughed off an old European consciousness and formed a new one underneath. After forty years of readings, prizes, lecturing, itinerant college teaching, four Pulitzer Prizes and nationwide popular admiration — Frost and Sandburg once shared a *Life* magazine centerfold — Frost suddenly became a poet meriting the serious attention of America's leading literary critics.

On March 26, 1999, James Collins, the American ambassador to Russia, hosted a Russian-American celebration of Frost's semisesquicentennial, recalling the astonishing trip of 1962 and Frost's world-famous poetry. There were readings and speeches — translations, encomia, eulogies. Among Moscow's literary stars, as I looked back over my shoulder at the trip and the last years of Frost's life, I saw how crucially Trilling contributed to the modernization of Robert Frost. At the same time, I felt I was again looking over Frost's shoulder as he, at the pinnacle of his literary life — the inveterate iconoclast, who had made a career of writing unconventional meters in conventional forms — was creating public history.

In his maddeningly distorted study of American literature, D. H. Lawrence remarked that "An artist is usually a damned liar, but his art will tell you the truth of his day. And that is all that matters.... Truth lives from day to day. Never trust the artist. Trust the tale." Of course, Frost was not a liar. That was Trilling's astonishing point. The real Frost, the important Frost, was not the poet with democratic simplicity of manner, the comforter of those embittered by modern life, the celebrator of old virtues, old pieties, old ways of feeling — in short, the grandfatherly Frost he had persuaded many of his readers to take him to be. The "real" Frost was the skeptical craftsman who made witty, half-serious remarks at the expense of the carefully cultivated, stereotypical figure:

"People who read me seem to be divided into four groups. 25% like me for the right reasons; 25% like me for the wrong reasons; 25% hate me for the wrong reasons; 25% hate me for the right reasons. It's that last 25% that worries me."

Trilling's speech turned that 25% around by pointing to the control of hollowness, disintegration and inner consciousness in such a perfect poem as "Neither Out Far nor In Deep." Henceforth, critics understood that Frost, putatively eclipsed by Eliot, Pound, and Stevens, was not to be set beside guitar-strumming Sandburg, booming Vachel Lindsay and timidly patterned Amy Lowell. All along he had been an orginal, modern poet whose figures, characters and images by their irony, by their separateness and self-reflecting isolation, by the seriousness underlying their modest humor and their often expressed tenderness, seemed reassuring only after first having overwhelmed a reader with their terrible intensity. Thoroughly contemporaneous, his poems were not allegorical and symbolical like William Vaughan Moody's or Trumbull Stickney's, his literal contemporaries. As Frost put it in the folksy way he had of punning on the vernacular,

"I can't hold with those who think of me as a symbolist poet, especially one who is symbolical prepense. Symbolism is all too likely to clog up and kill a poem — symbolism can be as bad as an embolism. If my poetry has to have a name, I'd prefer to call it Emblemism — it's the viable emblem of things I'm after."

When I look back on various poets' original intentions, I see that Frost, Pound, and Williams were similarly idealistic and American, and that Eliot and Stevens differed from them only in degree of social rhetoric.

Retrospectively, I see that Frost's literary canonization followed his role in the rehabilitation of Ezra Pound, whom he met in England on his first trip abroad. By chance, Alfred Nutt's widow had seen and accepted for publication *A Boy's*

Will, its title taken from Longfellow's "My Lost Youth." By chance, Harriet Monroe had asked Pound to be *Poetry* magazine's European representative. By chance, the English poet Frank S. Flint met Frost at the opening of Harold Monro's Poetry Bookshop on January 8, 1913 and insisted that Frost meet Pound. Flint sent Frost a calling card from Pound, giving Pound's address — 10 Church Walk, Kensington — and underneath the note: "At home — sometimes." When Frost appeared at the address a month later, Pound himself opened the door. When he learned that Frost wasn't bringing a copy of the soon-to-be-published *A Boy's Will*, he marched off with Frost to the publisher, fetched a copy home, and read it in Frost's presence. His long, enthusiastic review in *Poetry* launched Frost. He then lent the book to Yeats, who called Frost's "the best poetry written in America for a long time."

In 1914, Pound especially praised Frost's second book, *North of Boston*, for its "quite consciously and definitely putting New England rural life into verse." Pound's support led to Frost's connection with Holt publishers and laid the basis of his American reputation. Subsequently Frost went one way, Pound another; they printed negative opinions of each other's work; and after the Second World War, Frost concluded that Pound was a traitor justly imprisoned in St. Elizabeth's Hospital.

In 1954, *The New York Times Book Review* featured an excerpt from Pound's review of Frost's first book, along with a review by Horace Gregory of the *Literary Essays of Ezra Pound*.

This struck home. By August 1956, Frost was ready to do something to help his old friend. Chatting with Frost outside his cabin in Ripton, Vermont, a Marlboro College graduate Frost had taught said "there was supposed to be a poetry revival going on." Frost replied:

"I know nothing about that except the intellectuals and such are putting out a lot of paperbacks. Poetry some of it almost as prickly as Ezra Pound's.

They're not treatin' Ezra right down there in Washington, in the asylum. They're lettin' reporters and almost everybody in on him all the time, the beggars. *Somebody*, maybe the President, ought to create a fund so he could go to private quarters. The trouble is his kind of writin' is not the sort a President would read or have sympathy with."

Six months later, Archibald MacLeish, who had long been campaigning for Pound's release, asked Frost, who knew Eisenhower's White House chief of staff, Sherman Adams, to join Eliot and Hemingway in signing a letter to the Attorney General. Frost had his name placed at the head of the list and, after some shilly-shallying and a goodwill trip to England, a lunch with Adams, and a dinner with Eisenhower in the White House, Frost joined MacLeish in securing Pound's release and dismissal of the indictment against him.

With almost dramatic irony, Frost's role in rehabilitating Pound coincided with similar Russian efforts on behalf of venerable friends and the cultural tradition. People like the poet and critic Kornei Chukovsky, the musician Mstislav Rostropovich, and the physicist Pyotr Kapitsa helped to safeguard the lives and to restore the reputations of poets like Akhmatova, scholars like Oksman, and novelists like Solzhenitsyn. Despite ideological hostilities and Cold War rhetoric, outstanding intellectuals in both countries were moving toward a common goal.

Trilling's critique added great weight to Frost's literary figure; the reading at Kennedy's inaugural assigned him a vaticinal role; and Pound's rehabilitation emphasized his achievements as a mediator. Given the nature of world politics and new possibilities for social and intellectual exchange, wasn't it up to him to establish peace between the two great, antagonistic nations by stressing their common cultural heritage?

Frost's concept of Russia, however, was like most Americans'. All art and literature produced in the Soviet state was Russian, and all Russian literature was a congeries of footnotes to Tolstoy and Dostoevsky. Russia was one vast union extending from Vilnius to Vladivostok, speaking one dominant language and ruled by one central authoritarian government. Power that had been concentrated in the hands of a tsar was now concentrated in the hands of a different autarch, who, though head of the Party and head of the government, was but a man and, therefore, approachable. How customs and laws differed from one part to the next or how native populations regarded central, omnipotent Moscow Frost had no idea. In the Forties, Russia had joined in defeating Germany; in the Fifties, Stalin had died; and in the early Sixties, coincident with Kennedy's inauguration, Nikita Khrushchev's government seemed to be relaxing. Newly bohemian painters and wildly popular young poets who gave readings in football stadiums, old-line socialists and aged revolutionaries who had survived the labor camps and been rehabilitated, everyone said that the government was becoming mildly liberal. In 1961 there had been widespread reports of open elections to be held in Party cells. Frost himself believed that the grand old Russian state was humanizing.

Looking back, we can see how, after the thirty years from the beginning of the First World War to the end of the Second, the early Sixties were a special time of extraordinary ebullience when everyone acted from the conviction that political reform was coming and that Beauty, Truth and Good were about to triumph. In America, McCarthyism had faded; *Brown vs. the Board of Education* offered new hope to Blacks; and Kennedy's patronage of the arts moved cultural activity to center stage. In Russia, political repression eased, experimentation dominated the theaters and the art galleries, and Khrushchev indirectly but officially blessed re-examination of the past. Frost's view of the world rather accorded with "Caesarism," the doctrine that at crucial historical moments, great men, drawing popular and mercantile support around themselves against a stultifying ruling class, move a nation forward, often by violence. Though he clearly preferred Caesar Augustus to Julius Caesar, Frost was certain that an accord between Russia and the United States could be achieved at the highest, personal level. Through his friendship with the White House chief of staff, Sherman Adams, he had gained access to Eisenhower. Through his friendship with Stewart Udall, who wanted to study poetry, he gained access to Kennedy. Kennedy drew the connection closer, allowing Frost to go see Khrushchev to participate in achieving an accord.

Frost was always teasing about his political position, much wanting to live to 1976 in order to be half as old as his country, and early on asserting that the beauty of Socialism was its putting an end to the individualism that cried out 'Mind your own business': "Terence's answer would be [that] all human business is my business." In old age, Frost had transferred the burden of his poetry from his verse to himself. More than ever, he came to see himself as a cultural activist.

Frost was and was not the President's ambassador. Domestic rehabilitation in Russia allowed increased foreign contact. The Lacey-Zarubin agreement of 1958 established artistic and academic exchanges between the United States and the USSR. Thanks to the enthusiasm and skillful diplomacy of Anatoly Dobrynin, the Russian ambassador in Washington, in the early summer of 1962 an exchange was arranged between Frost, the leading, living American author who was part of the world, classical tradition, and Alexander Tvardovsky, the leading Russian poet-editor, famous for his wartime epic *Vassily Tyorkin* and his thaw-time satire *Vassily Tyorkin in the Next World*. Kennedy knew very well who Frost was and wanted Frost to embellish his entry to the highest office, just as he wanted the office to enjoy and to encourage American culture. In order to reach his goal, Frost needed presidential sponsorship. Long a romanticizer of Virgil the *vates* and an admirer of the political role of that faithful, learned countryman, he keenly felt the special blessing laid on him by his presentation at the Kennedy inaugural. Some days he himself was persuaded that he was the living symbol — *the* bearer — of American tradition, America's greatest poet. To many people every day he was. Because he tantalizingly suggested that he traveled with a message for Khrushchev and returned home with a message for Kennedy, the apparently ambassadorial aspect of his journey remained. Health problems and then political problems prevented Tvardovsky's visit from taking place. Frost died in 1963; Tvardovsky, in 1971. The exchange was never completed, but the effect of Frost's half — Part I — was momentous.

Frost believed that Americans were one people. Because he supposed that the Russians were one people, also, he had no sense of the extent to which continual scarcity and surveillance had riven the state. He rather assumed what Walter Benjamin had written in 1928 — that the Russians had "already performed unimaginably difficult tasks, and built up, against the hostility of half the world, the new system of power. In admiration for this national achievement all Russians are united." Frost's own, self-appointed task in bringing the American and Russian peoples together was to poeticize their international relations. After all, for him, both as man and artist, poetry was the great overthrower of separateness.

To the Russians, white-haired Robert Frost seemed the incarnation of their Santa Claus, *Ded Moroz*, or Grandpa Frost, the jovial New Year's spirit. They knew nothing about Trilling. They adored the homespun, New England poetry. And they knew that President Kennedy honored him and had sent him over. In translation, his poetry conveyed an image of a pastoral America comparable to their romantic vision of their own vast land. They remembered Sergei Yesenin as a poet from the village, one who was lionized as "the people's poet," and forgot how he had turned against his own lyricism and at the age of thirty hanged himself, leaving behind such lines as:

> *In this world all of us are bound to vanish;*
> *The copper color of the maples slowly dries;*
> *Blessings on you, Heart, forever for showing*
> *Up to flourish and to die.*

They knew that Frost presented a pastoral landscape, but they did not know that, like Yeats, Pound and Eliot, he had expressed ever darker themes as the long war years brought violent change. To them, the idiosyncratic verse with its New England idioms and dialect, which had developed into a tight iambic of canonical forms and the loose iambics of colloquial speech, seemed natural. Those who knew any of Frost's commentaries were delighted to believe with him that:

> The poet goes in like a rope skipper to make the most of his opportunities.... The freshness of a poem belongs absolutely to its not having been thought out and then set to verse.... A poem is the emotion of having a thought.... The only discipline to begin with is the inner mood.

Like the American reporters covering Frost's trip, the Russians in general kept reading Frost superficially and extracting narrow political meanings where none was intended. For example, as part of his projection of New England pastoral, Frost read "Mending Wall," which begins: "Something there is that doesn't love a wall." The papers played this as adverse criticism of the Berlin Wall, which made Frost unhappy, who had had no such intention.

The Wall has been gone for a decade now. In the course of the last forty years, Russia's political features have changed and its world standing has plummeted. Its economy has been carpet-bagged to death. Lakes have been polluted; forests have been clear cut; acres of farmland have been irradiated or poisoned with pesticides. Ignoble, unsuccessful, colonial wars have sapped the morale of its military. Lack of proper maintenance makes its submarines sink and its airplanes crash, as if all its machines were operated like the high-axled trucks of forty years ago, their parts held together by bailing wire. Still, Russia sends men into space. There are more and more cars; in the morning and late afternoon, there is rush-hour traffic. There is food in the stores — many delicacies for those who can afford them. Young women in the capital cities are stylishly dressed. Young men, too, follow the latest, world-wide fashions. People speak freely not only in private but also in public, and, depending on how much money they have and how good their connections are, they print, stage and film what they say. To be sure, the threat of censorship again hangs over the country like a low, leaden cloud, but *economic* repression has changed everything, including available literature. The rise of crass commodification in Russia, as in America, has turned books into verbal entertainment to be sold for profit. Quality poetry and fiction are only a small portion of what reaches the public. First-rate work is hard to find.

There would now be no point in a Frost-Tvardovsky exchange. There is no politician on either side who represents national authority, and there is no poet who bears a national emblem. Some Russian writers have taken a stand against the oligarchs, and some Americans, against corporate financing. Many on both sides, however, have simply tucked their heads in the sand — or, like some of the Russian "stars" from the Sixties, gone abroad or joined the dominant forces. Freed from political censorship, Russian poetry today makes no strident protest. The struggle for justice and egalitarianism that has long characterized the Russian intellectual world continues, but a blend of the old ideal and the new, sophisticated forms is only beginning — a David ready to hurl his five stones at the Goliath of the market place. The once-promising era that brought the release of Pound, the rehabilitation of great Russian writers, and Frost's vaticinal mission has not borne fruit. Never mind that now good poets' "kind of writin' is not the sort a President would read or have sympathy with," today's presidents simply don't read.

Still, there are artists who follow the old ways, and many people who follow the arts. On my March 1999 reading-and-lecture trip to St. Petersburg and Moscow, the grand poet Bella Akhmadulina and her husband Boris Messerer invited me to the Bolshoi's revival of Rodion Shchedrin's ballet based on Yershov's *The Little Humpbacked Horse*. Messerer's sets sparkled with the colorful flair of folktale patterns. Guided by the little gray horse, Simple Ivan traveled through the imaginary realms of the Firebird, Heaven and the Underwater Kingdom, turned into a handsome prince and married the princess. The music was charming; the dancing, graceful, sometimes witty; the set, spectacular. Messerer caught "the possibility of realizing secret fantasies hidden in the theme of this beloved fairy tale, of giving free expression to the ironic subtext." Backstage after the performance, the magical kingdom, the rows of glittering church spires, the elaborate throne, the ornate flies, the arching horses in precious mosaics on the huge scrim — all came apart and were wheeled off on palettes. 'Which was real?' I wondered; 'the beautiful, longed-for kingdom, or the wood-and-cardboard sets, like a Potemkin Village being stacked in a warehouse?' The everyday world is poor and dull. The world of the imagination is as gem-like and enticing as ever. Now in Russia — no less than ever before, I think — the difference is astonishing.

As I look through photos of forty years ago, reread old Russian friends' notes and letters and dedicatory inscriptions in their books, the past recurs with vivid poignancy. Those *were* special times because those were *special* people, creative artists and critics who had endured humiliating censorship, painful imprisonment, destructive warfare, and unending, heartbreaking loss without losing faith in their culture and dedication to the freedom of mankind. Their moral strength was exemplary. Their joy in being alive was uplifting. Their impatience for the better future that they were certain lay ahead was energizing. They were grand men and women — all the grander for working together in the same place at the same time. Sometimes I forget how much I miss them.

Looking around now, I, too, see that out of the life we have, art creates the life we want. The holy fool, the fantasist, the poet dramatize the sacrifice by which our intelligence protects our innocence in a world that is, at worst, hostile and, at best, indifferent. Looking back, I see that by playing local, verbal games Frost renewed the loyal skepticism of *our* culture, persuading us and anyone who would read him to agree that

> *It takes all sorts of in and outdoor schooling*
> *To get adapted to my kind of fooling.*

That brief period in the Sixties that promised so much now seems far away. From the comfortable vantage of our present security, however, when we look we can see how much we have lost. Frost's trip to Russia was his last, great contribution to our common history.

Robert Frost in Russia

MONDAY

One evening in May 1962, Robert Frost and Anatoly Dobrynin, Soviet Ambassador to the United States, dined at the house of Stewart Udall, Secretary of the Interior. Out of that evening came the proposal for a cultural exchange between the two poets, one American, one Russian. In July, President John F. Kennedy requested Frost to be the American participant. Frost accepted, and details of the exchange were soon arranged, for Udall himself was going to Russia in late August at the head of a delegation to visit hydroelectric installations.

Frost asked Frederick Adams, director of the Pierpont Morgan Library in New York and a friend of long-standing, to go with him. I was asked to go along to help with arrangements and the language. The assignment was unusual for all three of us. Frost had traveled to England and Israel in recent years, but he hadn't been abroad very much and never under such authority. Adams, as a leading librarian, had dealt with many people of various persuasions, but never with Russians in their own country. And I, though I had been to Russia and though I remembered Frost personally in a hazy, boyish way — he had taught our English class one day twenty years before — had never been a cicerone, much less aide to such a man.

On Monday afternoon, August 27, 1962, we were to get together at the State Department to go over plans for our trip. By bus and train I came down from the Pennsylvania mountains that morning. I walked into the meeting and met Adams for the first time. Frost had declined to attend. There was, in fact, no need for him to be there, for what we discussed concerned details that Adams and I were to look after. Adams had been seeing Frost off and on all day about arrangements. The Soviet Exchanges Staff of the State Department had gone to much effort to prepare the trip properly, to help make it as comfortable for Frost as they could, and to be sure that he would have with him in Russia any books he wanted and any help he might need. They expected him to talk candidly, freewheelingly, any place and any way he chose. They even expected to be, perhaps, mildly embarrassed by his frankness. Like everyone else, they knew that Frost publicly teased the State Department and that he would say what he felt. They knew that Frost had been invited by the Russians — with the approval of the Secretary of State and at the invitation of the President — and that the State Department's role must seem to Frost supernumerary. At the same time, they knew, as Adams and I did, that without their organization, assistance, and encouragement the trip could not succeed.

The meeting this Monday took place in a modern office. The floors were vinyl, and the furniture was steel and plastic. The room we sat in was on a long corridor of countless doors punctuated by water coolers, red EXIT signs, and stainless-steel elevators. It seemed peculiar that the road to Russia lay through such an impersonal forest. Most of the Russian offices I had seen were high-ceilinged, had dark wood paneling, Victorian desks and green baize-covered tables, lamps with green glass shades like inverted cake bowls, and worn, worried Persian-type rugs on a wooden floor. We had come here to Washington to do business and, without ado, did it. The men we talked to were cordial and full of hope for the success of Frost's visit. They were modest about their own part in it.

An hour or two later, Adams and I drove with Secretary Udall to his house for dinner. Mrs. Udall greeted us. Frost was waiting for us.

"Hello there, Freddy," he said to Adams. "You all set for our adventure?"

"Robert, I'm ready for anything you are."

Adams and Udall introduced me to Frost.

The weather was hot. We took our coats off and turned to talking about the next day and the trip itself. The Udalls' children moved casually and happily among the guests. It was an informal family evening.

As it turned dark around nine, small children were put to bed. Times and places of meeting the next day were agreed on. Lunch at Ambassador Dobrynin's was confirmed. Mrs. Udall moved among the company with skilled poise, saying how much she, too, wished she could go to Russia. And Udall reminded Frost and the rest of us of what the trip promised in cultural understanding and cooperation, of how important it could be in helping to shape a fresh, peaceful attitude between the Russians and ourselves.

Frost was excited, of course. He spoke of his expectation of meeting Premier Nikita Khrushchev, of his desire to talk straight to him, to tell him, "right off, this and that." He said he had just one favor to ask the Premier, but he wouldn't tell us what it was. He was saving it, he said. That was what he wanted to talk to Khrushchev about. Khrushchev would know what he meant, if he really was the kind of man Frost thought he was.

I didn't know. I wasn't at all sure that Frost would achieve what he had in mind. I was sure that the Russians would much like and admire his spiritedness and the integrity of his convictions. I felt certain that they would venerate him as a great literary man. I could guess that he would be met at the airport with bouquets of flowers and welcoming speeches. But I had doubts about his getting a political message across. Later that evening, as I thought still on what Frost had said, I began to wonder if the "real" Frost would get across, if Frost wouldn't remain for the Russians only a symbolic image of a stereotyped and rapidly disintegrating American myth. And the more I thought about it, the more clearly I came to understand that the success of "our adventure" depended almost entirely on Frost himself. If he could successfully communicate to Russians the substance of his poetry, he would "win." Everything depended on that.

TUESDAY

The next morning we met in the black-trimmed lobby of the Jefferson Hotel and crossed the street to the Soviet Embassy. Frost, the Udalls, Adams, myself. Three or four young men in gray-blue double-breasted business suits jumped into action, like amateur actors caught by surprise when the curtain goes up and their backs are still turned to the audience. This way, that way, here, please — and we were up in Ambassador Dobrynin's apartment, where we were to lunch. The ambassador, his wife, the cultural attaché, and an assistant met us. The ambassador, who, with Secretary Udall, had initiated the trip, prepared to send us off cordially and with enthusiasm, certain from everything said that what seemed to the travelers a hazardous adventure would be in everyone else's eyes a conspicuously successful public event.

Frost admired the ambassador and was charmed by his wife. The conversation at the table was light but serious; in a word, urbane. There was no artificial patriotism, no notion that cultural contact was an aspect of international party politics. Frost thanked Dobrynin for having been instrumental in arranging the trip, expressed his pleasure in traveling with Udall, reported that the President was sending him, complained about the ineptitude of the State Department, kept saying he was going over to have his preconceptions confirmed or corrected. Born in the district of San Francisco called Russian Hill, he was "going back" to Russia, he said.

The ambassador repeated his high esteem for Frost's poetry, assured him that it was well known in Russia, that ovations would greet him everywhere. He said that he personally had informed his home office of Frost's arrival time to make sure that he was met.

It was a pleasant, slightly tense, yet gracious lunch. Red French wine and Armenian brandy were served. The conversation turned to cultural and social change, to the America of the 1920s, to vodka vs. bathtub gin. Frost had never made any, he said, but, sure, he'd known people who had, though there's not much of it any more, he added. He asked if they did that kind of thing in Russia.

Dobrynin smiled, his eyes sparkled, and he said that they couldn't because there weren't enough bathtubs to go around.

Everyone laughed. Frost spoke later of his respect for Dobrynin's wit and candor, for the integrity which, he felt, lay behind the ambassador's public gestures. The Russians are all right, he mused, if they send that kind of fellow over.

The Russian part of the trip started at the Dobrynins'. Three or four months later, when Frost lay ill in the hospital,

Dobrynin remembered him with get-well messages and a message of congratulations on the occasion of the presentation of the MacDowell Medal. The poet who was more than a poet had met an ambassador who was more than an ambassador. Each in his own way carried his country in himself with dignity and pride.

Frost's trip was an exploration, a high-minded game between his poetic and political selves, just as it was an exchange between two countries with different ideological schemes. As Frost was leaving the lunch, the ambassador's wife wished him a calm and successful airplane trip. With a mischievous gleam in his eye, Frost quipped, "Thank you, it's going to be some adventure. I guess I can't ask you to say a prayer for me, though, or wish me Godspeed, because you don't believe in God." "I wish you a good journey from the bottom of my heart, which is better," she replied.

Outside on Sixteenth Street once again, looking back at the embassy, the house George Pullman had built as a wedding present for his daughter in 1912, we were jarred by America. For all the speed of planes, which have brought Moscow only a dozen hours away, they seemed incongruous intermediaries keeping Russia from us. After all, we had just had lunch in Russia.

Frost remarked on this as we crossed back to his hotel. He was going to lie down awhile now, take a little rest. Yes, he was all packed. "Come up to the room at three-thirty," he said.

"Got to be ready in time." He paused. "It's all right so far, isn't it?" he said. "Let's see what the rest of it's like."

By six-thirty we had driven to the airport, Frost had talked to the press and waved good-by, and we were curving slowly up in a lazy arc to follow the coastline northeast and then head out across the Atlantic.

Everyone was ebulliently tense. Udall's group and ourselves were flying over together. The engineers teased each other, pretended the Baltimore power station we were flying over was a Siberian installation, said that a young bachelor among them would have to do a Cossack dance with the stewardess.

"Do you like airplanes?" Frost had asked as we walked down the corridor to the loading ramp. "No," I had said, "I used to have a license, but I like ships much better." "Yeh," he said in the specially deprecatory, nasal way he said "Yeh" when he wanted to twit or to protest an institution, "Yeh, I always get a little scared. You never can be sure it's going to work."

He sat now leaning back in his seat, staring straight ahead with vacant blue eyes, his hands together across his stomach, his mouth slightly open. Every few minutes he would give a start, turn to Adams beside him, and check on a detail — had he sent a note to so-and-so, where was so-and-so now, did they get the books off? For a brief spell he was resting, relying on people and a machine he did not know and could not trust, refusing to be reconciled to reliance. As the flight wore on, he relaxed a little. He dozed. But the plane's vibration disturbed him, and the sense that the adventure had really begun aroused him. He hardly slept all night. He kept bringing up images from his past, kept referring to accomplishments and obligations, trying to take his own measure before strangers would take it, before he would be taking theirs.

Adams was calm, confident. Occasionally he glanced out the window. He would talk to Frost of old friends, joke with him about Russia, as if going to Russia were nothing more than going to, say, Denver. He was bright-eyed, thin-lipped, with an aquiline nose, casually accurate, gracious, intellectually strong, loyal, and sincere. He was reading before dinner.

Later Frost said to me, "You know, Freddy's a real aristocrat. Related to Roosevelt, too. That's all right. They don't have any like that over there, do they?"

"No aristocrats," I said.

"Yeh," he said, "it's all workers and such. Yeh, I knew that. Though I bet you they have some. You got to have aristocrats."

The blonde stewardess came into the cabin. The young bachelor, rehearsed by the translator traveling with them and beefed up by applause and general chuckling, made, in hopeless Russian, a presentation of a flower from his dinner tray and a protestation of undying love from his heart.

Twenty-four hours had passed since our adventure had started, and we were flying eastward fast. By the time our families at home were in bed, we were breakfasting in London.

Wednesday

It was past midnight. The cabin lights were out. Their shoes off, their collars unbuttoned, the sleeping men seemed to have been dumped at random into their seats.

Frost was sitting up forward by the window. He said he never could sleep on planes, he was too nervous about it all.

"It's a grand adventure, isn't it," he said, "this going to Russia, I mean. Crazy too. At my age going all the way over there just to show off. That's what we're doing, isn't it, just showing off. You think they'll understand us? They ever read my poems?"

"Sure, they have," I said, "especially the very popular ones."

"'Birches?'"

"'Birches,' 'Stopping by Woods.' I think 'The Death of the Hired Man' has been translated too, and 'Mending Wall.' That was one of the first. They started translating you before the war. And a lot of them know English. They're studying it more and more. If you give readings there, probably most of the audience will understand you right off."

"Languages. I never did do much about them. Oh, I could read the classics all right, you know, but I never got more than a little French. Never needed them. It's different with you fellows now. They study a lot over there?"

We talked about words and what you do with them, how a poet puts them to work, makes them sing.

"Every poem has its own little tune, you know," Frost said. "That's the way it comes to me, as a tune. You got to know how to do that, say it so you get the tune, too. Rhyme. You can't do it without that. Most of the time. You got to know how to take care of the rhyme."

And he told about a man, middle-aged, successful in politics, who confessed to Frost that, above all, he wanted to be a poet but was a bit shaky on the rhymes.

"I asked him," Frost said, "where's he going to get them, Mother Goose?"

His own career had been shaped by diligence and luck, he said, and he started recapitulating it that night as we sat there in the darkness of the dormitory-like cabin of the jet airplane high over nowhere.

He recalled his years in England most vividly of all. He was once again coming back to England, and going beyond. He and his family had moved there fifty years before. He had taken a little farmhouse out in the country in Buckinghamshire, committed himself to being a poet, met Thomas and Abercrombie, and yet never dared presume he would succeed. He was just trying it out, as he put it. He had to find out. He did not go to Paris, did not visit Europe at all. He seldom went anywhere, he said, stayed there at the place in Buckinghamshire and later in Herefordshire with his wife and children, wrote, saw friends. His poems, he knew, were not like those most poets were writing. It was just a chance, just

31

luck, he said, that he met an editor of *O'Connor's Weekly* [*sic*] and, through him, Alfred Nutt's widow, the first editor he sent them to, who championed them. She took his second book, too, the following year. He had been writing poems for over twenty years then and had enough for three or four books, he said.

"Ezra Pound likes them," Frost said, "he helped me. He was my friend. You know, I got him out of there," he said, meaning the hospital in Washington. "He was a good poet. You couldn't just leave him there. That was awful, what happened to him. I knew a lot of them," he said, "I knew just about all of them."

He remembered his two years in England with special affection. It was there, then, that he passed from obscurity to recognition, that he became the sort of man he wanted to be, that he was first called a "poet." He remembered the labor and the luck. At the height of a long career, at a time of conspicuous public activity, he well remembered how he had been unknown, the values he had lived by and the things he had come to value. Despite his wide popularity, he kept coming back to awareness of his own aloneness, of how he had really to stand himself against himself. The public's acclaim, which, like any artist, he required, could never be trusted to make the apt definition of talent. After all, he seemed to be saying, it's you who have to write the next poem. He was annoyed that he and Sandburg were linked in the public mind. Yes, he admitted, he himself had helped create that image by allowing articles on them both to appear side by side, as in *Life,* but he disrespected the public for accepting the likeness. He did not like Sandburg's politics — he thought them naïve — and he did not admire Sandburg's verse. When someone asked him what he thought of Sandburg's first book called *In Reckless Ecstasy,* he paused for a moment and then said, "Carl's got no brains. That's why he can be ecstatic."

His prejudices were deep. He often scorned the very people who were helping him, both because their help was a limitation on him, an imposition which, no matter how he needed it, he also had to detest, and because he was certain that their help was seldom disinterested. He never wrote a review or an article on a living poet's work, he said, never played that game at all. "I never wrote a review in my life," he saide, "and I'm not going to."

In the politics of poetry he had won first place though he eschewed the easiest way, though he insisted on preserving an integrity of position as, with words, he insisted on an integrity of diction. You may want to say immediately that he could easily eschew reviews and avoid the literary world, because the literary world eschewed him. Though he was known as a poet, he was admired by some people after the success of his second book, in general writers, critics, and intellectuals in America then, as in Europe now, regarded his poetry condescendingly, left him to college teaching, readings and adoration by clubs of middle-aged ladies. Suddenly, a few years after the Second World War, his reputation in the Anglo-American literary world began to grow. Men understood him not as a semi-sentimental regionalist, a sort of leftover Georgian poet, but as a witty, trenchant, almost metaphysical lyricist of extraordinary dramatic intensity.

He was almost forty before he could publish a book of poems. He was about seventy-five when the literary people who could understand his work started doing so. He had played an odd, peripheral role in the politics of poetry, and then suddenly, admired everywhere as one of the four or five major poets of the twentieth century, he was catapulted, almost literally, by his poetry into politics.

At the Inauguration of the President in 1961, he recited what he called his most patriotic poem, a poem he read in Russia, too. But he felt he had failed at the Inauguration. "It was the wind and the sun," he said, "the glare. I couldn't see a thing," he excused himself to himself with words other people had said. But he came back to that reading several times. "It's like the fellow who fumbles in the big game," he said to me that night in the air. He paused.

"But everybody said the glare was too strong," I said.

"That's what they all said, sure sure," he added. "I was ashamed."

He wanted to succeed. He wanted to be perfect. He was that proud. So he required the approval of people he did not respect.

We landed in Moscow at five. A delegation of Soviet writers met Frost. Alexander Tvardovsky was there, poet, editor of *Novy mir* (New World), and a Lenin Prize winner, who was to have visited the United States soon after Frost's return but who never came. Alexei Surkov was there, poet, secretary of the Writers Union and one of the key figures in the administration of the Soviet intellectual world. Yevgeny Yevtushenko was there, slim, confident. Mikhail Zenkevich, a poet, and Ivan Kashkin, a professor, were also there, the men who published the first Russian translations of Frost in their 1939 anthology *American Poets of the Twentieth Century*. Although the Russians were obviously not yet sure of their guest and of what to make of him, they were polite and dutifully attentive. Frost was much wearied by the long plane ride. Arrangements seemed to be in the hands of two women, specialists in American literature, from the Foreign Section of the Writers Union.

Yevtushenko had to duck out early to keep another appointment. There was a press conference in the airport waiting room. But despite the gray weather and Frost's fatigue, you could sense a special and optimistic tone in the Russian intellectual world. As the saying goes, they had put their best foot forward. Here was Tvardovsky, the man most responsible for engineering the success of the liberal *New World* in which, two months later, *One Day in the Life of Ivan Denisovich* was to appear. Here was Surkov, who in 1960-1962 temporarily assumed a new position sympathetic to the intelligentsia by having edited a little volume of Pasternak's poems and the first volume of the new *Concise Literary Encyclopedia*. Here was Yevtushenko, world famous, whose "Babyi Yar" had caused a sensation the year before and whose politically electrifying "Stalin's Heirs" was to be published six weeks later. These men, along with Zenkevich and Kashkin, had come not only to greet Frost but also to express their allegiance to those independent, humanistic values expounded in Frost's poetry, which they were trying to make operating principles in their own new literature.

Greeting Frost, they greeted the West of their own cultural tradition. For them, Frost personified this tradition. Frost's most important accomplishment in Russia was not the political embassy he aspired to but the enactment of freewheeling literary activity which he, by his poetry readings and by his talk, encouraged among the Russians. Won by the Russians away from some of his preconceptions about them, Frost was an example and a reminder to them not of the politics of literature but of vitality of the literary tradition. Yevtushenko, for example, who had not stayed for the whole conference at the airport, subsequently invited Frost to dinner and talked to him informally several times. Sharply criticized in late 1962 as a self-aggrandizing showoff, in January 1963 Yevtushenko sent Frost a simple, sincere telegram: TODAY I'VE READ AGAIN AND AGAIN YOUR POEMS I AM HAPPY THAT YOU LIVE ON THE EARTH.

The initial press conference at the Moscow airport was a

one-sided skirmish. I had the feeling that the Russians were respectful to Frost's eighty-eight years but were expecting a version of Carl Sandburg, who had been in Russia the year before and had gone around playing his guitar.

"I'm here to talk with you about science, art, athletics, great music and, of course, poetry," Frost said. "We admire each other, don't we? Great nations admire each other and don't take pleasure in belittling each other. Petty, small talking down."

The Russians smiled blankly, like round moon faces in a receiving line. They looked trapped. They looked bored. The correspondents kept asking Frost questions, Frost kept answering, the two guides were bustling around, nervously watching every move everybody made as if afraid some guest would in displeasure flee from their tea party.

"You've got to have power to protect the language, to protect the poetry in it. You've got to be strong to protect poetry. Poetry's the most national of the arts, not so much painting or music. A great nation makes great poetry, and great poetry makes a great nation. It works both ways," said Frost.

The Russians didn't understand him. They understood the words, of course, but you could see by their expressions and by the ladies' nervousness, and you could tell by the fact that no Russian responded to Frost except in platitudes of welcoming and good-wishing, that they could not comprehend what Frost meant by the national character of poetry or by the use of power to protect poetry. Whatever they may have dimly sensed was his meaning, their own experience of both nationalism and political power in relation to poetry was so different from Frost's that what he said was baffling. Besides, it would be better to wait a little and see how things would go. You had the impression that these people knew Frost by reputation, that whoever had read his poems understood them in terms of the image of the poet the old reputation had created.

"Yesterday the well-known poet Robert Frost arrived in Moscow from the United States," said the note in the Moscow newspaper. There was nothing of Frost's comments at the airport press conference, about rivalry, his quip about the Russians overtaking America — "If the Russians beat my country in everything then I'll become a Russian" — his ambassadorial presentation of credentials — "Russia used to own the West Coast of the United States, California. That's where I was born. I was born in Russian territory. There's a hill in San Francisco called Russian Hill. I was born right near there." None of the Russians responded to Frost's remark that when a poet doesn't get enough money he gets a job like anybody else. "Same here?" Frost asked, but no one picked him up. The guides assured him that Russian poets had lots of writing to do and published extensively. Frost talked about his career, about all the odd jobs he'd had when young, "just to earn my bread and butter," he said.

He was extremely tired and seemed wearied, also, by a

feeling that he wasn't getting across. "Sometime I'll go a little deeper into our approach to each other," he said. "I've got some rather bald things to say."

Someone asked him if he wouldn't find it hard to communicate because of the language barrier. Frost retorted with a smile, "We all laugh in the same language."

Our suitcases were put in black, Buick-like Zims, and we drove to the Sovietskaya, a hotel now reserved for important foreign delegates but once the site of the Yar, a famous restaurant with gypsy entertainment. Terry Catherman and Jack Matlock from the Cultural Section of the American Embassy had met Frost's plane. Matlock stayed on to dinner in the hotel. Frost was pleased to have him there and pleased that he was with him most of the trip. He liked his forthrightness and admired his ability. Surkov and Tvardovsky had also gone to the hotel with Frost to see that he was installed. Talk in the car was still exploratory, but Tvardovsky shot out one sharp witticism. Frost didn't yet understand who Tvardovsky was or what he did; he knew only that Tvardovsky was the "other half" of his exchange. Some one explained that Tvardovsky was editor of *New World.* Tvardovsky quipped, "Yes, I'm not only a poet myself but also a strangler of young poets." Frost was much amused at an editor's laughing like that at himself, and everyone, after the first moment, took the quip as harmless banter. To some of us it seemed sharp, for we couldn't help remembering how *New World,* under Tvardovsky, had been important in liberalizing the literary world of Russia. When you think back on what happened to artists and writers during the winter after Frost's visit, the irony of Tvardovsky's quip cuts still more deeply.

The guides wanted to discuss a list of proposed projects, excursions, voyages, tours, and inspections. Before leaving Washington, Frost had indicated he wanted to see Khrushchev's birthplace at Kalinovka, near Kursk, and go to Tolstoy's estate, Yasnaya Polyana. As we talked together on the way over, it had become clear that he really wanted to see Khrushchev himself much more than his birthplace, and to read poetry and talk to living, leading writers rather than take an all-day drive to see Tolstoy's grave. We all agreed that Frost was too tired now to go anywhere or make any decisions. "Let's decide it in the morning," we said. "He ought to have dinner tomorrow," I said, "if it's possible and convenient, with Chukovsky or Paustovsky, both of whom he'd much like to see." Both were senior writers, about eight and fifteen years younger than Frost, with outstanding reputations, Chukovsky as critic and children's writer, Paustovsky as essayist and major novelist. The guides said they didn't know anything about that, they'd have to see, we could discuss it tomorrow when we discussed the whole program. "There isn't much time," I said, "and we must arrange things so Frost sees some people and reads his poems. He doesn't like just sightseeing and staring at monuments." Tomorrow, we agreed; we'd discuss it all tomorrow Yes. Fine.

Tomorrow.

Secretary Udall had gone with his group to the National Hotel direct from the airport. The guides had cleared out. Frost rested a bit. Adams unpacked. I made some phone calls. Matlock came back, and we four had dinner. Matlock brought us up to date on plans for the stay in Russia, what had been going on, what seemed to be coming next. We looked over the August issue of *New World*, which included several new translations of Frost's poems, published this month in honor of his trip. We kept saying how much the Russians admired Frost's work and all he represented, how successful and how busy the trip would be.

We were in high spirits, nervous, uncertain. Having had a dinner in our hotel, we felt anchored to our adventure. Frost was extremely tired when he went to bed that night but full of enthusiastic wit in anticipation of what lay ahead.

THURSDAY

For the next two days the business of being the leading American poet as an official guest in Moscow nearly overwhelmed us. Adams finally said, "Robert, no more interviews. You haven't given yourself a chance. You're exhausting yourself and not doing what you want to."

On Thursday before lunch we had a drive around Moscow. We sat in the same well-worn black Zim. We swung through the parking lot in front of the hotel and headed back toward the center of Moscow along the Leningrad Highway.

Moscow is laid out like a wheel. The hub is still the old citadel or city fortress, the Kremlin, on the bank of the Moscow River. The river cuts through in a broad, flat V, as if tracing the hands of a clock in a jeweler's window up from the 4 to the center and then out to the 8. A series of avenues forms the first ring, limning the inner city. The Garden Ring marks the one-time city limits. You're reminded that the city gates used to be on it by the names of the wide squares where Ring intersects to the wide radial streets leading to other cities, to Yaroslavl, Leningrad, Kiev. Still farther out, about twenty miles from the center, lies the new highway encircling the city, a white cement ribbon far beyond the city's houses and factories, waiting for the city to move out and occupy the dusty land it rings.

Many buildings have been added to Moscow, but the basic plan has not changed in five hundred years. What used to be the financial and business center almost in the shadow of the citadel is still full of commercial and economic-planning offices. The entrance to the big department store GUM is on Red Square. Hotels, movies, concert halls, theaters — both the Bolshoi and the Malyi — the offices for deputies to the Supreme Soviet, the old part of the university (now the humanities and social sciences section), and the Lenin Library — all lie in a semi-circle in what you'd call a stone's throw of the Kremlin itself. Some streets have been renamed and renamed; others still carry names that contrast sharply with the present. Just off Red Square, no distance from the Bolshoi, the subway stop is called Hunter's Marketplace. The English Club on Tver Street became the Museum of the Revolution on Gorky Street, but stone lions still guard the carriage entrance and exit, and upper-class Muscovites still refer with pride to the building they associate now not so much with the barbarities of the land-owning nobility as with the luxury and grandeur of a way of thinking and living consciously European. Despite change, the historical monuments remain and are well cared for (in Leningrad, even more so). Much of the strength of the present comes, it seems, from the visible remainder of the past.

On our drive around town, we cut behind the Kremlin, passed the old university and the Lenin Library, went out Kropotkin Street with its elegant, early nineteenth century town mansions, past the huge swimming pool (where the Palace of Soviets was to have been, but the land was found to be too soft), out along the river, across it, and up to the new university buildings atop Sparrow, now Lenin, Hills. We got out of the car and looked back on the city, from the Maidens Convent Cemetery in the foreground to Sokolnik Park hidden behind the city in the distance, dominated by the gold cupolas of old churches and the miniature Empire State Building spires of the hotels and offices of the Stalin era. On the way we had passed a number of two- and three-story houses, some stuccoed with tile roofs, each set on a large and separate lot and surrounded by high wire fencing. "What are these?" Frost asked. The guides said they were just workers' homes, people's homes. Actually, they were reported to be residences and guest houses for very high party and government officials. Somebody said that Mikoyan lived in one of them. They commanded an exhilarating view of the city.

We drove back down Lenin Avenue past the Donskoi Monastery, now the Academy of Architecture, and the main building of the Academy of Sciences, once the mansion of Count Gregory Orlov, Catherine the Great's minister and lover, in the vast Neskuchny Park overlooking the Moscow River. We crossed Revolution Square and went through the old bohemian section of the city directly opposite the Kremlin, crossed the river, went up and through Red Square past the mausoleum and the crenelated wall, out Gorky Street and back to our hotel. Surkov and Tvardovsky joined us for lunch.

Frost had spent much of the morning giving interviews and discussing plans. Matlock had come in at ten to report on what the embassy was planning and to say that steps had been taken to secure an interview with Khrushchev. Along with Valentin Kotkin, secretary of the administrative office of the Foreign Section of the Writers Union, an efficient and courteous man, one of the guides showed up at eleven to work out Frost's schedule for the remainder of his visit. She wanted Frost to follow the protocol her office had already drawn up, a list which included much of what Frost had no liking for: sightseeing. We reminded her of Frost's age, of the shortness of the trip, of the many people to see and talks to have. We were insistent. She politely relented. And she announced that that evening we were to dine at Paustovsky's. The following night we would be at Chukovsky's.

We lunched at a long table in the hotel's second-floor dining room. Matlock was with us; the other guide had come with Surkov and Tvardovsky. All along Frost publicly supported the idea of cultural exchange and its putative accomplishments, although at first he privately doubted its efficacy or value. At the beginning of his Russian trip, what he was told about Russia tended to alienate him from it and to keep Russia in his mind as that collection of prejudices, misconceptions and fantasies which is any man's notion of a distant and foreign country. Some Russian officials were insensitive enough to try to give Frost the stereotyped Intourist image of Russia with rugged women, noble men, giant industry, vast agriculture, wholesome living, hearty entertainment, heroic history, and lovely new garden-apartment homes. On the other hand, the Russian press was playing up Frost's visit. Translations of his poems were cropping up almost daily in the papers, often four or five an issue. Poets were writing encomiums. Tass was reporting everything he did. With some officials, on the one hand, trying to keep an accurate image of Russia from Frost, and the press, on the other, publishing translations and quoting his comments on labor and goodwill and the primacy of language, it seemed at first that the Writers Union and the politicians were out to use Frost. By the end of the trip, however, this had changed. Frost had become convinced that cultural exchanges were the one means of effecting some sort of genuine understanding. He had changed his mind because of his visit to Khrushchev, because of his successful poetry readings, and because of his conversations with half a dozen outstanding writers who, though the political situation in Russia in the spring and summer of 1962 had worsened, spoke up, and spoke Frost's language. Political pressure on intellectual activity was beginning to be repressive, but certain breakthroughs had been made. Writers and poets were still hopeful of moving constantly ahead with de-Stalinization of the intelligentsia. Nobody anticipated the setback which came the following winter.

Lunch in the hotel with Tvardovsky and Surkov was an *obed*, a five-course dinner served about three in the afternoon: hors d'oeuvres, soup, fish, meat and vegetable, compote, coffee. There were Georgian wine and Caucasian mineral water. The conversation was informal but general. There was much small talk, comparison of copies printed of a book of poems in the United States and in Russia. Tvardovsky and Surkov joked with each other. Nobody opened up. The lunch seemed a satisfaction of an official obligation rather than the pleasure of three senior poets.

After lunch Frost rested. He locked his door from inside so no maid or reporter could wander in and promised not to answer the phone. He felt he was beginning to establish a routine for the trip and that the trip was going all right, didn't we think so? Yes, we did, and I added that I thought tonight would be a very good evening. We would see the city apartment of a successful writer; it would be a man's house and would give an impression sharply contrasting with the image of the country derived from a hotel room.

From outside, the Sovietskaya looks like Russified 1930s modernism. There's a kind of dreary ornateness about it, a pretentious use of limestone and marble. In the lobby, you're struck by the lifelessness of the mottled marble columns, as stolid as elephant legs, the overstuffed leather armchairs, the rose-plum carpeting with borders of floral designs on a chocolate background running infinitely right down the hall and up the stairs in front of you. Usually the carpeting is covered with a white runner. The maids, the bellboys, the waitresses, the manager — the servants — move around singly. The Arabs, the Chinese, the Americans — the guests — move around in groups. Frost would walk up to the second floor, and the *dezhurnaya,* the maid on duty in her white apron, a starched fillet on her head, would hand him key 207 from her board.

He would pad audibly down the hall to the last door on the left. He would open the heavy chocolate-colored door, drop his hat on a bench in the vestibule inside, hang his overcoat in the closet, turn around and walk into his living room, a large room with French doors onto a tiny balcony. There were several overstuffed armchairs and, in the center at the round table, four dark, straight chairs. A carafe of water and two overturned glasses stood on a glass tray in the middle of the table. A desk, a chair, a table lamp were in one corner. There was a phone on the desk, an inkwell with purple ink and two straight pens, and, under the glass desktop, a hotel notice about laundry, tours, theater, telephoning. The bedroom was to the left: a wide bed with the blanket-in-a-jacket which serves as sheet and quilt, a dresser, straight chairs and a suitcase rack. The low lamp beside the bed was covered with an elaborately rigged green glass shade. The first night he was there Frost undid the construction and removed the shade so he could see to read; the next morning he proudly showed us his handiwork. The bathroom was off the bedroom. There was no view from the windows of the rooms, for there was nothing to view. The bedroom and living room looked out on the street and the parking lot in front of the hotel. You could watch workmen building an apartment house diagonally across, and you could see the tops of trees down the Leningrad Highway leading out of town.

Paustovsky, to whose apartment we went for dinner that

evening, lived in a large apartment complex subdivided into a series of wings, each with several separate entrances. The house was on a street running along the bank of the Moscow River. Tvardovsky lived in a different wing of the same building, where we came back for our last evening in Russia.

Two things struck me as we entered the Paustovskys' living room from the hallway: the table and the books. You had an immediate sense of tranquil, cultured excellence. As in most Russian town apartments, the living room is the dining room is the library. There were books to the ceiling all around the room. The room had a sofa, which probably doubled as a bed, a stuffed chair or two, a radio-Victrola, two or three tables with lamps, a footstool, and the big, oval table surrounded by five or six heavy mahogany chairs plus four or five more chairs fetched from other rooms for this special dinner.

At the Udalls' we had dined informally in American style. At the Dobrynins', we had lunched formally in diplomatic style. On the planes we had eaten from trays, airplane style. In the hotel we had hotel-style service — slow and impersonal, though the director in the beginning and at the end paid particular attention to Frost's group. (After the papers announced that Frost had met Khrushchev in Gagra, the hotel service improved noticeably.) Now, for the first time, we were in a fine Russian house, soon to sit down to an elaborate Russian dinner. Linen napkins, the embroidered tablecloth, the sprats on the table, the marinated mushrooms, the dark bread, the soft gray-black caviar, the salt herring, the salmon and sturgeon, the radishes, the plate of tomatoes, a beet salad, the small, sweet cucumbers, bottles of Georgian wine, liqueur glasses for vodka — the brightness of the table and the enthusiasm of the hosts made you confident that an evening of good food and warm, sincere conversation lay ahead. Frost was several times invited to Russian houses, and each time his host's hospitality pleased him deeply. By the end of the trip he was worn ragged from all he had done, and the last dinner was very nearly too much for him. But at the beginning he was fresh and eager. The evenings were good.

If you think on who was meeting whom, across thousands of geographical and political miles, you must say that those evenings were astonishing successes. You would have hoped for, but not have expected, so much easy, affable talk, such obvious mutual admiration. Frost gave public thanks on television: "Before I say anything about poetry, I want to thank my Russian hosts for their friendship and the good times they've given us. The exchange of poets between countries is more useful than the conversation of diplomats," he added, the morning before he received an invitation to meet Khrushchev; "it brings kindred spirits together."

Frost was meeting men of his own generation and inclination. Konstantin Paustovsky, at seventy, was one of the outstanding Russian novelists, considered by many people the leading independent-minded Russian prosaist now living. He had been in Italy the year before. In the difficult winter of 1962-63 that followed, he was to speak out bravely in support of the excellences of modern Russian literature against its censorship-minded detractors. He and Frost chatted amiably, through the translators. The ladies' voices would go higher and higher until Frost would pull away with a shrug and a sour face, ask for a résumé, eat something, and be caught up in the conversation again. He and Paustovsky spoke of their habits as writers and of the values they supported by their writing. Frost referred to the need for isolation and independence. Paustovsky said that he had a little house in the woods where, like Thoreau to Walden, he went in order to be alone with nature.

His family listened closely. His wife and daughter served. An old friend of his added to the talk. This was S.M. Alyansky, an art historian, the publisher, right after the 1917 Revolution, of the Alkonost Press, one of the outstanding publishing houses of modern Russia. It specialized in poetry, helping a number of important poets at about the time when Frost himself was beginning to win recognition. Alyansky's career, knowledge, and old-world charm made his presence that evening not only appropriate but also significant. I'm sure that Frost was not aware of Alyansky's merit. The guides tended to hover over Frost, as if ringing him off from imaginary autograph seekers; they themselves never initiated what administrators call "an exchange of ideas." I hadn't expected Alyansky to be present, and I couldn't have briefed Frost. Afterwards, when I told him who Alyansky was, he much regretted not having talked to him at length, though they had exchanged a few light witticisms across the table.

That evening, like several others, was memorable because of its tone rather than anything else. Of course, you seldom assume that a dinner party will provide headlines, but the spectacular characteristics of Frost's trip may make you presume all he saw and did there was some political insight or politically significant comment. His poetry readings and remarks to newspaper reporters were not infrequently interpreted that way. But the success and charm of the private evenings followed from the public unimportance of them. Frost and Paustovsky talked together most of the evening.

They agreed on the vitality and essential nature of centrality of purpose in both life and literature. They talked about their early, pre-literary years, when each had worked at odd jobs and knocked around his country. Frost said he had often jumped freights, riding in open box cars. Paustovsky smiled and said yes, he'd often done that, only he could go Frost one better: he'd ridden on top of the box cars. They laughed. Both emphasized a number of times, with fondness, that that time in their lives had always meant much, that it had shaped, if not what they had written, at least the attitude out of which they had written.

After dinner, the daughter put some Bach on the Victrola. Alyansky talked to Adams about art books and book publish-

ing. We left with the feeling that, for all the difficulty of talking through translators from the viewpoints of different national cultures, the Russian literary world at its best was as
bright, as gracious, as spunky, and as energetic as our own.
Frost said how grateful he was to have had such an evening —
he was obviously pleased, and he had made a hit — and Paustovsky
expressed delight at what he called Frost's "lyric energy."

More than thirty years ago, Paustovsky published a story
called "Moscow Summer" about the courage and integrity of
an imaginative architect, Hoffman. I thought of the story that
evening, and I think of it now, with Paustovsky attacked politically once more, and Frost dead. The story ends:

It was a hot summer. A smell of burning hung over the spotchy
clearings and dried-up swamps. The roads smelled of dust and tar. In
the woods the birches were already turning. Taking a shortcut, Luzgin
went straight across a clearing.

In the woods in the middle of the autumn-colored birches he
caught sight of Lyolya. She was coming to meet him. Shadows ran
over her face and her light, rustling dress. She rushed toward him.
The heat broke. Lyolya brought freshness with her, a vague happi-
ness, a breath of fall, vast spaces, the excitement of their recent love.
She seemed to be coming from the land where the clouds had been
smoldering.

Luzgin stopped, overwhelmed.

"You're here." Lyolya came quickly up and gently squeezed
Luzgin's hand.

"Lyolya," Luzgin said hurriedly, "Hoffman . . ."

"Yes, I know." Lyolya calmly glanced up straight at him. "He's dead. I got a postcard from his father. So. Now that he's dead I can't get some very silly ideas out of my head — I don't know why. He died well. He taught me not to be afraid of life."

Luzgin, listening to her, was watching the clouds. It seemed to him that, beyond the smoky haze, he could make out the enormous country which Lyolya had just come from — a country pellucid in the air and the shimmering sunlight. Our wild and dreamy ancestors must have imagined the golden age to be just like that.

FRIDAY

Frost asked for breakfast "on time." I went to order it, after having made him promise not to let anyone into his room except Adams or me. Interviews were scheduled for right after breakfast. But less than ten minutes later when I came back, Adams was standing outside Frost's door saying, "Guess what." Frost, in a white shirt open at the neck, was giving an interview to a Russian reporter and waiting for coffee, milk, grapes and raw eggs. We all breakfasted; Frost talked. Then the reporter left. For a moment we three were by ourselves, but Frost so quickly cited the reporter's politeness and interest, which was certainly true, that Adams and I could only make a weak joke about it all. Frost seemed puckishly pleased that he'd changed his mind and fooled us.

A moment later, the scheduled reporters appeared along with the guides and Kashkin, Zenkevich and young Andrei Sergeyev, who had also published translations of Frost's poems. The interviewing went on until lunch.

Frost planned a tentative program of readings and translations to be taped for television the following week. He gave reporters his impressions and opinions and suggested what he believed the import of his mission.

The *Literaturnaya gazeta* (Literary Gazette) published its interview the next day:

The renowned American poet Robert Frost is in the Soviet Union. Yesterday he gave an interview to this paper's correspondent, M. Tugushev. Frost was 87 [*sic*] in March. As a man who knows Frost well aptly said, it takes a great life to create great poetry.

"Mr. Frost, every American schoolboy reads your poems. Tell us what you yourself think is poetry's place in the life of a nation."

"Poetry's essential for everybody, for it lives in every person. And therefore it's close to them. Take curly hair. Maybe it's naturally curly, or maybe artificially. You've got to distinguish in poetry too."

In the next question-and-answer, one sees the difficulties of being quoted in a language one doesn't speak. The *Literary Gazette* correspondent, like most Russians and Americans coupling Frost and Sandburg in his understanding of poetry, asked

Frost how important popular recognition had been to him. The reporter talked about recognition by "the people" or "the nation." Frost replied that he had considered himself a poet only after other people had called him one. The guide, who was translating Frost's interviews, erroneously turned "other people" into "the people," and Frost seemed to have come out with a party line statement on art:

"What do you think is the meaning of popular recognition to a poet?"

"I never called myself a poet until the people did. At first I was very embarrassed by it. The word 'poet' is the greatest praise. Young people often call me up and introduce themselves, 'I'm a poet.' To my way of thinking, that's immodest. There's got to be respectful fear of that word, because after all it's just like saying about yourself, 'I'm a good man.'"

By comparing what this interview says Frost said with what one has read by Frost or has heard Frost say, by being aware of the sort of questions and answers quoted here, one gets from this interview a fair impression of the image of Frost which preceded him to Russia and which some Russians cultivated. For Frost fitted both camps. One group read him as a witty, testy, independent artist who, by his life and writings, like Ernest Hemingway, appeared as a champion of the social autonomy of the creative person. The other group read him as the darling uncle of the people, an anti-intellectual, venerable

Cincinnatus of the Western literary world whose roots were deep in the America of the people.

Robert Frost is not only a remarkable poet. He is also a teacher, an adviser to young poets.

"An adviser precisely," he emphasizes. "You see, I never studied the craft of poetry myself. And by the way, in classes I never read my own poems and never let them be used as models. People often come to see me and we talk about poetry."

The interview even became involved in the struggle going on in the Russian intellectual and artistic worlds between the liberals and the conservatives, a struggle focused sharply on the work of the young poets. None of us realized, until the interview appeared in print, that in a small way Frost had been enlisted on the conservative side. In answer to a query, he gave a little speech about the tune in a poem being its essence, about his hearing the tune as rhythm and rhyme. This was turned into a flat statement supporting conventional metrics.

"You're a poet of traditional form. You prefer that to free verse?"

"Free verse, too, can be a regular part of poetry, but I like rhyme and rhythm better."

On a number of public occasions, Frost was queried on what he knew was a double-edged issue: work. He couldn't come out against it, yet to support work in general, he knew, would be merely to utter propaganda. Now, as at other times, he parried the question by making a kind of pun on the Soviet emblems of labor, joking that his symbols were bigger and sharper:

"We know you're not only a hard worker in the field of poetry. You like physical labor, too?"

"Yes. Work — that's the chief thing in life. I never was an ivory-tower scholar; I always liked the soil. And there was a time I made my living working on a farm. My favorite tools are the ax, the scythe and the pen. By the way, I just realized that there's a likeness between them and your 'Hammer and Sickle.' A sickle — that's a little scythe, and an ax is a sharpened hammer. One of my books, too, has the ax and scythe on the cover."

One of Frost's couplets goes:

Nature within her inmost self divides
To trouble men with having to take sides.

It's entitled "From Iron: Tools and Weapons," and in his poem "The Objection to Being Stepped On," which he frequently read during the Russian trip, he made a light comment on perverse uses of equipment. In the poem, he talks about having stepped on a hoe and been hit on the head:

But was there a rule
The weapon should be
Turned into a tool?
And what do we see?

The first tool I step on
Turned into a weapon.

In the newspaper interview, Frost's conversational paraphrase of that poem was made a statement that corroborated Russian political propriety:

"Nowadays I often think about the words 'weapon,' 'tool.' A tool can turn into a weapon. When the peasants would rebel, they'd turn their tools into weapons. I often hear that the atom has to become a tool of peace. But you must always keep in mind that it can also be a weapon of war."

At the conclusion of our conversation [the reporter continued], I said that Soviet readers knew Frost's poetry through translations published in anthologies, in the *New World* and in the *Literary Gazette*.

"Unfortunately we often read poetry in translation, and a good translation's so important here. I know your poetry, too, only in translation. Now, when I get home," Robert Frost jokingly observed, "I'll study Russian so I can read your poems in the original."

At this time the *Literary Gazette* was still a leading liberal newspaper. Several people, perplexed at the interview, asked me if Frost had really made such propagandistic statements, and I said no, but that it was very hard for many Russians to grasp what Frost was really saying, that they tended to miss the nuances, to misunderstand his play of mind.

Sunday's issue of the newspaper *Literatura i zhizn* (Literature and Life) included translations of three Frost poems and three paragraphs about them which gave, through that anti-liberal paper's language, a notion of the conventional Frost the conservatives wanted to see. The poems published were "Hang On Until Morning" (in English, "Good-by and Keep Cold"), "On the Dunes" ("Sand Dunes"), and "The Dried-up Brook" ("Hyla Brook").

Robert Frost, the dean of American poets, has come to visit the Soviet Union. He has gone through life's school of hard knocks. During the long years of farming his land he slowly developed both his orchard and the tree of his poetry. Many winds and frosts broke and felled branches, not only in that orchard but also in his creative work. But Frost persevered and attained honor and recognition. His own experiences in life gave birth to his appeal to hang on as long as possible.

Knowing by experience the burden, and sometimes even the risks and dangers of labor, Frost celebrates the pertinacity of the fishermen in their struggle against the sea's caprices on the dunes along the shore.

He is interested not in the external, ostentatious side of things but in their inner value and beauty, and another time he will patiently wait until the brook which to others seems to have dried up again starts babbling. The stream of his poetry has flowed on unceasingly for over half a century already.

The publicity may have been pleasing — as Sterne once cracked, "I wrote not to be fed but to be famous" — but the image it conjured up was small help to the real Frost. He was made into a grandfather of poetry. Because of the great difficulties in language his poems were frequently translated into homiletic rhymes. The wit and the conceits of the original became moralistic or aphoristic phrases of advice on living. "Good-by and Keep Cold" begins:

> *This saying good-by on the edge of the dark*
> *And the cold to an orchard so young in the bark*
> *Reminds me of all that can happen to harm*
> *An orchard away at the end of the farm*
> *All winter, cut off by a hill from the house.*
> *I don't want it girdled by rabbit and mouse,*
> *I don't want it dreamily nibbled for browse*
> *By deer, and I don't want it budded by grouse.*

The Russian translation, called "Hang On Until Morning," faithfully follows the meter and the rhyme-scheme of the original, but, despite the translator's effort and knowledge, the imagery is changed beyond recognition:

> *In winter at night as I go off to rest*
> *I think of my orchard beneath the white snow.*
> *How defenseless it lies in its open place!*
> *In what shape will I find it after dawn?*
> *There's always fresh worry every day:*

> *A deer may bite off the tasty buds,*
> *Or a hare will gnaw at it in the spring,*
> *Or I have to smoke the caterpillars out.*

The last two lines of the original:

> *. . . Its heart sinks lower under the sod.*
> *But something has to be left to God.*

Become transformed into:

> *Trees, I know, have so many scares,*
> *But somehow God has to show them his care.*

During his trip, Frost used the leverage of popularity, won even through this kind of Wordsworth-and-Kilmer translation, to project a keenness of intellect and affection for independence which pleased his listeners and established for him a fresh and proper reputation among many Russians. Those who knew some English responded instantly. Able, literary men, such as Zenkevich, who translated Frost's poetry and were preparing an anthology of it, helped to form intelligent understanding. But it was Frost, above all, who by quick-wittedness and adventuresomeness won his audience himself.

Frost sensed a special kind of democracy in Russia, although, because of the language barrier, he could seldom act on it. Pretenses to communism aside, relations among individuals in Russia have an equality, an urgency, an immediacy about them which makes each day eventful and gives the person who lives through it a sense of achievement. For all the talk and the programming of socialism, people in Russia feel themselves very much individuals. They are proud and energetic, nationalistic and idealistic. They argue with warmth and love with ardor. They expect life to be confused; one's consciousness of vitality comes from the game of straightening it out. So much remains to be done that each man can believe in the necessity of his contribution to bringing the good life at least a little closer. Discussions of the meaning of life are serious, and art is as socially apt today as it was one hundred years ago. We, in our country, tend to pay attention to modern Russian writers in direct proportion to the noise of attacks on them. We know their classics well. The Russians, who know our literature less well, tend to pay attention to our contemporary writers who most completely and vividly dramatize for them what they consider the basic values of life. Their overwhelming favorite and much admired American novelist was Hemingway; among the living, they prefer J.D. Salinger and John Updike. For, they insist, life has a happy ending. They turned to Frost enthusiastically once they understood that he "understood," that out of the questioning and aloneness came affirmation of the goodness and ultimate triumph of man.

Frost was hesitant both to accept the Russians' admiration and to acknowledge the status and the energy of the Russian intelligentsia. He was loath to separate intellectual speculation from politics. At breakfast this Friday morning, we had chatted about the evening before and had gone on to discuss the social function in Russia of the writer and of the intellectual. Frost refused to regard the Russian intellectuals differently from the American, most of whom he considered liberal sapheads, casuists, brain pinchers, men of small faith and less courage. A few days later, however, he had imperceptibly changed his point of view. He didn't share many of the convictions or attitudes of the Russian intellectuals, but he acknowledged their integrity and activity. He became aware of the fact that in Russia to be an intellectual is to do something.

Late Friday afternoon we drove out to Peredelkino, a village about twenty-five miles outside of Moscow on the Kiev railroad. Before the Great Patriotic War a writer's colony had been established there, a number of wooden summer houses (*dachas*) built, and a central *dom tvorchestva* (literally, house of creativity), a pension, set up where many Moscow writers could spend three- or four-week vacations with colleagues, writing in the morning, walking in the afternoon, attending readings, recitals and dinners in the evening. Some of the best-known writers in Russia lived here. Pasternak's house was on the edge of the field in front of the Pioneer camp, looking across to the hillside cemetery where he lies buried and to the railroad station beyond. We drove out to Kornei Chukovsky's for dinner.

The square buildings, the baggy clothes, the foreign language, the unexpected food, the different manners — much of Russia was wholly strange to Frost. He had had no idea how different Russia would be. But the trip to Peredelkino, like the ride from the airport past a stand of birch, reminded him of land he knew and gave him a sense, by the tangibility of its imagery, of things close to what he had long lived by.

Chukovsky's two-storied frame house with many windows, a glass-in porch downstairs and an open sun porch upstairs, was set among tall, dark pines behind fruit trees and a vegetable garden. The green wooden gates were open. We pulled into the drive in our Zim, and Chukovsky came quickly out to meet us. He greeted Frost warmly and with poise in fluent English.

A spare man with bright eyes, straight white hair, and bouncing humor, he had spent three weeks in England in May. He had won a Lenin Prize and had received an honorary doctorate from Oxford. There was light banter that, though Frost had received an Oxford doctorate in 1958, four years before Chukovsky, Chukovsky had received his at the age of eighty, four years younger than Frost. After we had glanced through the children's public library near his house, Chukovsky, famous for his children's verse as well as for literary criticism, put on his red and gray Oxford gown and, as he said, danced like a jester. He and Frost reminisced about England, and Frost quipped, with the deliberate frugality of a Vermonter, that he liked the degree all right but hadn't bought the costume.

We walked through Chukovsky's garden and withdrew to his study upstairs while his daughter-in-law attended to dinner. The guides had come with us, of course. Chukovsky had invited the writer Max Polyanovsky, the poet Stepan Shchipachev, and the critic and scholar Julian Oksman. Shchipachev was then head of the Moscow section of the Writers Union, a white-haired lyric poet quiet in manner with easy charm and an attitude toward poetry that encouraged younger poets to fresh experiments. Oksman, in his middle sixties, one of the most brilliant literary specialists, moved and spoke with dynamic energy. Chukovsky's acumen and style, his erudition and unusual knack for the apt gesture, set the tone of the evening. I, for one, was delighted to be with these men whose wide learning and social consciousness gave me a sense of being, there in that summer house in the forest outside Moscow, in the midst of what is vital in the world.

At dinner Chukovsky was host, translator and cultured man of letters. He had seated Frost at the head of the table, Shchipachev on the left and himself on the right. A three-way conversation the Russian food and lyric poetry started up, Chukovsky serving as intermediary and commentator. The rest of us listened in.

One of the guides watched quietly from behind her plate, but the other, overzealous in her duty and, so it seemed to the rest of us, especially attached to Frost, started repeating Chukovsky, to everybody's embarrassment. Her voice went higher and higher; Frost, somewhat deaf, heard less and less. Suddenly she jumped up to run around and shout into Frost's ear. Frost darted back, and raised his hand to the side of his head. "Go away, sit down," he said, wagging his hand, "no, no, no, no, no." Having no idea why she had popped up, he thought she had suddenly wanted to kiss him. She sat down again, a bit chastened, and Chukovsky once more took up his central role in the conversation. Later, back in the hotel, Frost chuckled over the misunderstanding, but he was also annoyed. He was beginning to feel that the two guides were more of a hindrance than a help — and he recalled how, before the trip, he had rejected out of hand a suggestion that a woman translator go along with him. He was beginning to be fed up with all the incomprehensible buzz-buzz of Russian. He had enjoyed talking openly with Chukovsky in idiomatic English. He and Chukovsky had exchanged comments and wisecracks, had very much hit it off. This sharp reminder to him — pointed up by the events of the next day — that, despite the urbanity of his host and the excellence of the table, he was in the heart of a foreign land brought him up short.

The table was lavish and the guests in high spirits. We drank vodka and wine toasts, sipped tea and ate cake, felt almost at home. Many times later Frost spoke of his delight with the evening, told how Chukovsky had danced in his Oxford robes, and recalled how they had looked through his library together. A Tass reporter had appeared, gremlin-like, before we sat down to dinner and arranged another in what seemed an interminable series of interviews. But even this shadow of a public record didn't dampen the conviviality of the evening. The reporters, the guides, the well-wishers, the patriots — all stood between Frost and Russia, but nevertheless there were many moments when Frost felt as if he were touching Russia itself, and it was these moments — especially this evening — and his readings and the meeting in Gagra which Frost remembered as the essence of his Russian adventure.

SATURDAY

Children and other superstitious people say you must shriek "Rabbit!" when you pass a cemetery. It's supposed to be the first thing you do on the first of the month. We forgot to, for whatever reason, and all morning long we wished we could have undone our bad luck. The Russians, too, wished it could have been undone. They apologized later. But Saturday, September 1, came and brought with it one of the tours which our guides had arranged and Frost had agreed to.

The day was gray, raw, rainy. Everybody was complaining of the weather, of the cold and soggy summer. Several American newspapermen met us downstairs in the hotel after breakfast. It had rained during the night and was still drizzling. The sky was bleak. The wet asphalt and cement made the city look dreary. The streets were vacant.

After meandering half hopelessly though the dirt yards of torn-down buildings and new construction in a section of the city unfamiliar to our driver, we found Middle School No. 7, supposedly an "English" school — that is, a school which emphasized English and where work in the sixth and seventh grades (thirteen- and fourteen-year-olds) was conducted in English. We walked in hesitantly, and we felt all the more that we were intruders because of the confusion we seemed to have introduced. Clearly, we were only half expected, like the inspector-general in Gogol's play.

Frost had been reluctant to go in the first place, but some of his poems had been selected and translated for children, he loved his own grandchildren and the spontaneity of small people, and he, who had spent the evening before with Chukovsky, a poet-hero to Russian children, was conscious of the public aspect of the visit. From the first, though, he was apprehensive: would they understand him?

The headmistress was impeccable. You could sense that Frost instantly drew back from her. There were slogans and signs and English idioms about manners all over the walls of the corridors. An elementary class, which we visited first, was dumfounded by the appearance of this white-haired foreigner. After a few moments we escaped and, having looked in on a more advanced group, ended up in a section of the seventh grade.

The children rose to attention beside their desks when we entered. The girls were in chocolate dresses and black, everyday pinafores which Russian schoolgirls have worn for generations. The boys had on the blue-gray uniforms with mock brass buttons that identify schoolboys. All had the scarlet Pioneer neckerchief. The teacher wore a knit suit belted at the waist; her black hair was drawn back in a braided bun. She addressed herself to the class but especially to a redheaded boy in the front row, requiring them to ask Frost a question. Trembling, the boy asked, "What do you think of our cosmonauts' flight?" "Great," said Frost, "don't you think so, too?" "Of course," said the boy, certain he had done his duty but at a loss where to turn next.

Frost asked who would like to go to the moon. Slowly, very timorously, as reporters made notes and photographers took pictures, the children put up their hands. "You want to get away from here any way you can," quipped Frost. There was silence. "I'm kidding you," he added and tried to explain what kidding meant.

The teacher tested the redhead on his English. "What does *plavat* mean, Nikolai?" she said.

The boy hung fire, then stammered out, "Th-th-th . . ."

"No, no," she said, "try now."

"Thwim."

"No, no," she cried. "Not thwim, but," and she paused for effect, "sweem!"

We all shuddered slightly, embarrassed for the teacher and sorry for the boy.

The teacher asked Frost to recite a poem. He said a few lines from "Pasture." None of the students seemed to understand, and the teacher's insistence on explaining the lines, an effort that was identified but not translated to Frost, only made matters worse. Frost suddenly felt very tired from the attempt and suggested we leave. He exchanged polite good-bys with students and staff and, putting on his fedora and hunching up his herringbone overcoat against the raw weather, walked back to the car.

"That was a damned fool errand, wasn't it?" he said. We could only agree. Though the Russians later said that there had been a mistake in selection of the school, the trip was depressing. It made Frost feel all the more isolated and, sadly, even farther from his longed-for goal of seeing Khrushchev. For, he figured, if he was to spend all his time gabbing with school children who could hardly understand English he would never get South. And, to be sure, there hadn't been a word from the South itself at all.

Frost now wanted to be by himself, just Adams and me with him. When we went into the reserved section of the hotel dining room for lunch and he caught sight of a table of Arabs and a table of Chinese, he turned around and headed back to his room. "That's a bad prejudice of mine, isn't it?" he said as we walked down the corridor. "But that was a foolish, very foolish morning." He felt he had been cheated, and the Soviet propaganda, suddenly made visual by the guests in the dining room, seemed to him foul and meretricious. We ate lunch in his room.

Frost rested in the afternoon, and Adams went to the Kremlin with Sergeyev, one of the men who had translated Frost's poems. That evening we visited a café, invited by Yevtushenko.

It was the Aelita, and it stands on Oruzheiny Alley just off Mayakovsky Square on Gorky Street, where the famous and impromptu poetry readings had been held and where Yevtushenko had recited the full "Babyi Yar." When first opened, the café had admitted all comers, so I understood, but despite the advertisements of our guides, changing times had dictated a different clientele. Customers were now admitted through the Komsomol. The café was sedate, and there was no line outside.

The world inside the café, like the world inside a coffeehouse on MacDougal Street, was very different from what was going on outside. The décor and tone inside were modern, spare but tasteful. Couples in their twenties and thirties sat in groups of four to ten at tables around the room, half divided in the center by a wall, sipping wine or drinking coffee. Cafés don't serve liquor. At one end of the room a band played jazz. Frost and Adams and I seemed entirely out of place, although actually the evening had been carefully arranged. We all sat at a long table and drank white Georgian wine. Yevtushenko was our enthusiastic and generous host. His energy buoyed up everyone and set the evening going.

There were several reporters there. The two guides had come along. Matlock was with us. Besides Yevtushenko, Eduard Mezhelaitis was there, an older Lithuanian poet residing in Moscow who, from a middle-of-the-road policy, seemed to be political father and spiritual cicerone to these younger artists. A day or two after we had arrived, *Pravda* had published a piece on Frost by Mezhelaitis entitled "The Blue-eyed Cliff," an affectionate term for a venerable old man. The article reflected the public understanding of the import of Frost's visit. There was, also, Yevgeny Vinokurov, a heavy-set, silent, talented young poet. Andrei Voznesensky, round-faced with a wide mouth and bright eyes, perhaps the ablest of the young group, sometimes sat across from Frost, sometimes stood behind him, sometimes leaned against the wall at one end of the table. There was hubbub as we all crowded around the several tables that had been pushed together.

Yevtushenko constantly addressed himself to Frost. The two men were a sharp contrast. Frost, in old age, stooped; his body was heavy, his throat and neck had become full; he gestured slowly, stiffly. He was alert, all right, and full of drive, but he had no reserves of strength. Yevtushenko's seemed endless. He was tall and angular; he moved impulsively, talked intensely. He was nimble, spirited, conscious of his popularity and importance. He would propose a toast, drain his glass, and with his long arm hold the wine bottle out to fill everyone's glass. It was hard to know who he really was, how much poet, how much politician. Frost was unwilling to separate the poet in Yevtushenko from the politician. When, the conversation having turned to good people vs. bad, Yevtushenko said that there were fewer bad people but that they were better organized and that often, because of the extremes they go to, "they provoke us into doing good," Frost retorted, "Like killing them?" Yevtushenko was surely thinking of de-Stalinization, but Frost was not prepared to draw so sharp a line between good and bad. He turned abruptly to Yevtushenko. "Is it good to kill a bad man?" Yevtushenko let it go.

In the midst of out talk and toasts, our presence was suddenly announced over the loudspeaker, and Frost was called on to "say" a poem. Nobody was going to explain the poem. Nobody was going to translate it. Here he was in a café among poets and customers a number of whom knew English. The poem would be carried by its music. After a few remarks of appreciative thanks, Frost said "Stopping by Woods on a Snowy Evening." The applause was long and loud, more, I thought, for Frost's being here in Yevtushenko's company than for any understanding of the poem itself. But, after all, wasn't this what Frost had asked for? He was personification of a tradition and embodiment of the young Russians' dreams of their future. He was American; he was famous; he was a great poet.

Tuesday's number of the *Literary Gazette* carried a poem by Yevtushenko, transcribing some of the emotionalism and the sincerity with which this young group approached Frost.

"Robert Frost in the Café Aelita"

There's America the Pentagon,
there's America the raftsman!
There's America the showoff
like a second-rate farce.
There's the America of Frost
and that's not hot air!

There he is —
               aren't I right? —
with farmerish cunning.
Robert Frost
               is the President
of the real America!
And I know
               that by right
for his being so natural
all the grasses selected
him as the candidate.
These elections weren't like
the others at all.
He was picked by the florets
and the dew-covered glades.
The wheat was a voter,
and so were the woods.

And he got all the ballots
of the songs of the birds!
Like
              the essence of truth
he was born from the earth.
He was chosen by trees
and confirmed
                        by the rain!
. . . It's hot; the hall's jammed.
We're quiet, like children.
He's at the Café Aelita
reading us poems.
Gray-headed
                     he's speaking
not from a position of strength
but from a position of blue
above the green earth.
And without laying
                  it on
I simply toast
The Frosts still to come
and you,
            Robert Frost!

In fact, Frost was so far from this group of young men,
both by age and by culture, that their evening was held to-

gether by mutual awareness of its public and political nature. Frost was out to see everything; Yevtushenko was more than cordial. He seemed to be on top of the world. In the late summer of 1962 there was still obvious ebullience among the young artists, still confidence not only in the rightness of their work but also in its final prevailment. Frost's allegiance, and their alliance to his standard, could have signified a respectability helpful to them, as also to young Americans, in the future immediately ahead. But Frost and most of the young group were far apart. Frost had no political elasticity. He later noted in an unfinished letter that on the trip "the nearest anything disagreeable was with their most prominent poet of all, Yevtushenko, who had been to Cuba and found refreshment of the revolutionary spirit there in friendship with Castro, and may be coming here." Yevtushenko was mercurial, charming, at moments suddenly, if briefly, removed — almost aloof — and moving so quickly you weren't sure if he were real or not. He talked about the glory of Castro and the deep pity of loneliness, and Frost, who often said that politics was about grievances and poetry about grief, was confused. He could not trust the way that Yevtushenko seemed to him to combine them.

Yevtushenko had asked Frost to dine at his apartment after the appearance at the café. We drove out along the Leningrad Highway past our once-gypsy hotel to a little street beyond Aeroport where, in a new building with other writers and artists, Yevtushenko and his dark-haired wife lived in a small, three-room apartment. The living room was rather large. The walls were hung with abstract Cuban paintings and an oversized, white campaign button saying in black clock letters: I'M A BEATNIK. The furniture was modern. The apartment was attractive. Everyone called Yevtushenko by his nickname, Zhenya, including his wife, our two guides, and somebody who came to the door by mistake.

At first we stood around smoking, looking at the pictures, making small talk. Yevtushenko's wife set the table; some of us brought plates and platters in from the kitchen. Frost was seated at a table in a corner, Matlock beside him, next to Yevtushenko. The room was full of motion, words, easy laughter. Most of the people were young. This was a party.

Mezhelaitis was there, and Vinokurov, too. Voznesensky had excused himself — he had a radio broadcast. After dinner Robert Rozhdestvensky and his wife arrived, wearing dark glasses. Rozhdestvensky did not take his glasses off and hardly talked to Frost. Frost was enjoying himself among these vibrant, self-confident poets, but, I think, he more and more felt that their world was scarcely his. At any rate, when asked to recite a poem he firmly declined. He admired the young poets' energy but disliked the bravado, the showmanship, of parts of the evening. Yevtushenko's flamboyance, coupled with that pro-Cuban zeal which Frost later remembered, seemed to Frost suddenly artificial. Yevtushenko said he would recite his poem "Weddings," a musical and moving lyric about himself as a small boy during the war dancing until exhausted at the weddings of soldiers he knew would never come home. Yevtushenko started explaining his poem. His paraphrastic prologue became overly long, I feared. Yevtushenko caught my impatience and broke off. There was a tense moment as I explained that Frost was more interested in the music of poetry than in translated explication, that he was waiting to hear the poem. The poem has a strong rhythm and much assonance. Yevtushenko declaimed it, as if performing, tossing his head back, waving his arms, reciting in a highly emotional pitch:

> . . . *By now I'm worn to shreds,*
> *by now can hardly breathe . . . .*
> *"Dance, boy!"*
> *the despairing cry,*
> *and off I go again . . .*
> *My feet seem made of wood*
> *when I get back home,*
> *but from another wedding*
> *drunks*
>
> *come calling me along.*
> *My mother lets me go,*
> *and soon I'm at another,*
> *dancing squatting by*
> *the tablecloth itself.*

The bride is crying bitterly,
their friends are all in tears.
I'm scared.
　　　My feet won't budge a step,
yet I've no choice
　　　　　but dance.

With his long hair, high cheekbones and lean figure, intoning his poem with high seriousness, he seemed an incarnation of a typical image of a poet. And he emphasized the immediacy and integrity of feeling and power of the revolutionary spirit.

Mezhelaitis recited a poem, a longish one about an airman shot down in the war. Vinokurov read. As I remember it, he, leaning forward over the table, recited in a low, steady voice two short poems, one, with redundant rhymes, about a cold cellar turned into a bomb shelter, and one about becoming a poet:

"What do you do to be a poet?"
I once asked with the trust of a child.
I got long explanations of it
From everybody, who tried and tried:

"Now, you do this. But this you don't!
Be sure to read this. Make minutes count!"
All these instructions, like thick smoke,
Made my head spin.

> *But at some point*
> *I went out, and by a newspaper stand*
> *The sunlight danced on an icicle!*
> *And I spat on the ground. And ignored the advice.*
> *And that's when I wrote my first line.*

We went back to the hotel toward midnight. It had been a Saturday, all right, from the do-it-yourself failure of the morning to the gala reception at the café to the poetry-filled evening in the apartment of the most popular poet in Russia. "We painted the town red, didn't we?" Frost punned as he tossed his hat onto the chair in the hallway of his hotel suite, pale and very tired. But he couldn't get Yevtushenko and his politics out of his head, and we talked for another hour or so about "the poet" and "the mob," about a poet's relation to his audience and his responsibilities to his country. Frost kept coming back to the politics of poetry, to art as a way of understanding, and therefore, as an instrument of morality, though he didn't put it that way. He kept asking how Yevtushenko could seriously believe that rhymes and revolution went together. He joked about the differences between Russia and America, about his brand of religion and about his own habits of thought and behavior. And finally, ready to go to bed, he asked, with a touch of sharpness, then chuckled, "Have they got the right kind of Sunday here so we can rest up?"

SUNDAY

Sunday in Moscow, as in New York or Paris, is a special day. Most people don't work, though almost all the stores are open. Children have no school. It's a family day: cousins and grandparents get together for dinner; parents and children go to the country with a picnic lunch or go swimming and boating in the Moscow River. Women dress carefully; men put on pressed, dark blue suits. It's a holiday, without anybody's going to church.

We made it a holiday, too. Frost had been invited by the translators of his poems, Zenkevich and Sergeyev, to see *Swan Lake at* the Bolshoi. Adams also wished to go, but I, who had seen the Bolshoi's *Swan Lake*, asked to be excused. We agreed to meet back at the hotel in the late afternoon.

We expected Frost to be bored by the ballet, but Adams said later that he wasn't at all. Ryabinkina danced brilliantly, with grace and evident delight, Adams said. Frost had a fine time. After the ballet, which started at eleven, Frost, Adams and the two Russians had lunch in the Prague Restaurant, where they sat at a table near Vinokurov and Voznesensky, lunching with an American newspaperwoman. The newspaperwoman, apparently, came over and effusively kissed Frost. The others were more restrained. Voznesensky said he would see Frost that evening at dinner, but he did not come.

The day was cool and sunny. I had lunched with friends

and met some colleagues and ridden in the subway and on trolleybuses around Moscow through crowds just walking, talking, enjoying their city on a peaceful late summer Sunday.

At the hotel Adams and I chatted a while before waking Frost up to get ready for dinner. We were to be at Konstantin Simonov's at seven.

The building, the stairway gave no hint of what Simonov's apartment was like. From the outside, the stones were as gray, the stairs as dark as any other apartment house. The landings were bare; the walls, blank. But inside the apartment we saw at once elegance cultivated in modern style. We saw handsome imported furniture and specially carved moldings. We sat in Eames-type chairs and on foam rubber sofas. Blocks of driftwood and pieces of sculpture stood on low tables and on shelves around the room. An artist's tastes and a successful writer's income had made this apartment both cosmopolitan and comfortably Russian.

There was a roast for dinner, and a red Astrakhan watermelon for dessert. We drank vodka from stem glasses with no base — you had to go "bottoms up." Mezhelaitis was there, as were the guides. The Simonov's young daughter said goodnight shyly before going to bed. The talk was all light, mostly about the food and about Frost's trip. Simonov told a few jokes and said proper phrases about the artist's work and obligations. The evening was comfortable and pleasant, but except for the table, not one you'd remember. Simonov and his wife were gracious, but nobody *said* anything. It was much like a dinner in an American upper-middle-class suburban house.

We left early, for we were scheduled to catch the eleven-fifty Red Arrow sleeper to Leningrad. Each of us armed with a suitcase, we pulled up at the special taxi platform of the Leningrad Station: the guides, Frost and Adams, Matlock and myself. The train pulled out of the station. The guides vanished into their compartment. Frost bedded down. And Adams, Matlock, and myself, sharing a fifth of whisky that appeared, like a genie, out of a suitcase, prepared for midnight adventures. A friend of ours joined us, a distinguished scholar with a great sense of humor, and we talked about books and writers and drank with merriment. At one point the conductor poked his head in, threatened to send everyone to his assigned compartment, was persuaded to return when he had checked the rest of his cars. Soon he was back again, downed a tumblerful of whisky in one gulp, and never was seen again — by us, at least. We had a gay, bright ride, with serious talk and silly laughter. We went to bed happy and arrived in Leningrad, that royal city, as Frost called it, with high expectations.

MONDAY

A train going into any modern industrial city takes you through the gray outskirts of smoky factories and depressingly identical rows of workers' houses. The heart of Leningrad is still a showcase of history, but the outlying districts remind you that Leningrad is now one of the centers of Russia's electrical manufacturing, shipbuilding, and heavy industry. You ride for miles — kilometers, rather, or, in old Russian style, *versts* — across the flat Ladoga Declivity, over gray-brown fields and through the fir forest that covers most of northwest Russia. But, as in the rest of Europe, the edge of the city is sharply marked: you go suddenly from fields and little houses to apartment buildings and warehouses. And then, a few moments later, you're in Leningrad, in the Moscow Station. As the *Leningrad Pravda* put it:

Robert Frost, the dean of American poets, arrived in Leningrad yesterday accompanied by Professor Franklin Reeve and the Director of the Morgan Library, Frederick Adams.

Frost is properly regarded now as one of the leading contemporary American poets. From the moment of the birth of American realistic poetry in the beginning of the twentieth century, Frost's name was inseparably connected with the "Poetic Renaissance," the name of the literary movement of which Frost was one of the "Big Five" poets.

Literary critics rightly call Frost a worker poet, a poet of labor. Farmers, hired hands, woodchoppers, workers are the central figures in his verse tales. The poet is very familiar with the people he writes about: for thirty-eight years he worked as a village teacher, a farmer, a newspaper reporter, before he made up his mind to publish his first book of verse.

Frost's poetry is profoundly civic. In many of his works he reflects on the human worth of the simple laborer, on his creative energy and love of freedom. Frost can genuinely be regarded as a spokesman of the dreams of the progressive, democratic segments of contemporary America. The basis of his creative writing is philosophic reflection on the permanent grandeur of the laboring man, the humanistic idea of the harmonious and all-inclusive reconstruction of the world.

There's no doubt that this trip to the Soviet Union will give the great American man of letters a chance to become more deeply familiar with our way of life. And the Soviet reader in Leningrad will find it no less interesting to get to know this leading American poet.

Robert Frost came to the USSR at the invitation of the Soviet Writers Union. In Leningrad he was met by the writers A. Popov, N. Braun, D. Granin and V. Toropygin. Yesterday our guest went sightseeing in Leningrad and met Leningrad writers.

Today Robert Frost will meet representatives of the public of the city in the USSR Academy of Sciences Institute of Russian Literature (the Pushkin House).

The article came out the day after we arrived. It was on page four, with a photograph of Frost. The headline on page one, for a different article, ran: MAN MADE HANDSOME BY LABOR, with a photograph of a young, round-faced milkmaid in a kerchief who promised fine beef production. You could, I know, point to the incongruity, even irony, of news in American papers squeezed in among implausible advertisements and senseless fillers. What was silly about the story on Frost was its preposterous image of Frost, almost a campaign caricature. Frost, really, had only contempt for such silliness.

The *Vechernii Leningrad* (Evening Leningrad), in its brief notice of Frost's arrival published late in the afternoon that Monday, unlike the *Pravda*, the "Truth," told the truth:

Today there arrived in town the great contemporary American poet Robert Frost, who has been visiting the USSR at the invitation of the Soviet Writers Union. The 89-year-old [*sic*] poet is accompanied by Professor Reeve and the Director of the Morgan Library, Adams.

Frost and his companions were met at Moscow Station by members of the Board of Directors of the Leningrad Section of the RSFSR Writers Union, N. Braun, D. Granin, A. Popov, newspapermen and public representatives.

The American visitors will see the sights of the city and meet writers.

Tomorrow in the Institute of Russian Literature of the USSR Academy of Sciences there will be an evening of Robert Frost's poetry and a documentary film of the poet's life will be shown.

But before that evening came there was much to be done.

We arrived about eight-thirty in the morning. There were no schoolgirls in pinafores to greet us, butterfly bows on their braids and gladioli in their arms. There was no brass band,

and the mayor of the city didn't come. But writers and reporters did, cheerful if sleepy-faced, flashbulbs popping and much shaking of hands. By every definition, including the civic, we had arrived.

Half an hour later, after a ride down the wide, treeless Nevsky Prospect through the center of Leningrad, we were in the Astoria Hotel on St. Isaac's Square across from St. Isaac's Cathedral, two steps from the Moika River, a three-minute walk from the banks of the Neva itself. It was all first class.

Frost had hardly slept on the train. We had some breakfast in his hotel room and then he went to bed. I went off to help make arrangements for Frost's stay in the city.

Happy as I had been to see old friends in Moscow and to walk through that teeming, powerful city again, I was boyishly delighted to be back in Leningrad, a city that seems to me almost as richly beautiful as Paris, is certainly braver, and to which I, for some foreign reason, feel specially close. There's plenty of junk in Leningrad, as there is in all big cities, but there is also an elegance and a simplicity, left over from grandeur, which impresses itself on you. I think back on the city with affection. There are corners and alleys and piles of logs and boats on the water and monuments and numbers of people who suggest, by their culture and their turn of mind, that the Western world is one. As I walked along the Neva toward the Winter Palace, crossed on the Nicholas Bridge and roamed Vasily Island, here in this old capital city of Pushkin and

(left to right)
Alexander Tvardovsky, Robert Frost, Secretary of the
Interior Stewart L. Udall, and Yevgeny Yevtushenko at
the Moscow airport

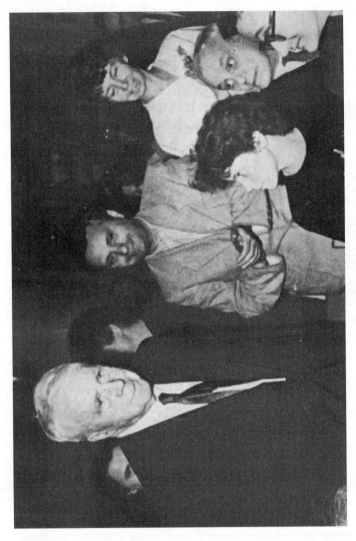

Frost entering Pushkin House in Leningrad for his first reading of the trip

Frost reading at the Foreign Literature Library. F. D. Reeve is at Frost's left; Alexei Surkov at his right

Frost on stage at the Café Aelita with Andrei Voznesenksy
and Yevgeny Yevtushenko

Andrei Voznesensky (smoking), Yevgeny Yevtushenko,
and Robert Frost at the Café

Frost visiting Middle School No. 7

Frost with the Matlock children; (from left to right) Hugh, James, and Nell

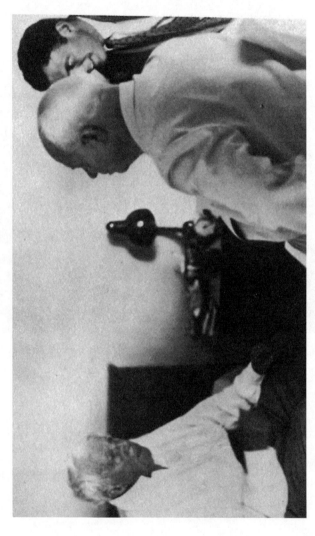

Frost meeting with Premier Khrushchev in Gagra; F.D. Reeve at Khrushchev's right

Dostoevsky and Blok, I remembered how, some time before, one Russian had ironically quipped when a conversation had turned to Frost and his work, "But our poets don't live so long." On that sunny morning, Leningrad seemed a city of radiant ghosts.

We all had a late, light lunch and went our several ways. I still had to get to the public library to arrange a visit there for Adams, and Matlock and I had agreed to meet by the Fontanka to take a ride in a public cutter, or sight-seeing boat, out onto the Neva and see the city from the water.

Frost and Adams, with Intourist guide and translator, had driven out to Peterhof to see the palace there. The Russians have restored it almost entirely; it was demolished by the Germans during the war. There are two palaces, really: the large, ornate eighteenth-century mansion built on top of a hill at the end of a long esplanade of fountains and surrounded by French gardens, and the little low-roofed brick cottage at the water's edge, Peter the Great's "Mon Plaisir." From the stone steps in front of the cottage, you look out to Kronstadt and across the bay to Peter's city itself. Back at the hotel Frost indicated he didn't think much of the palace or of the excursion. Adams said that Frost had been disgusted with the place, that he had remarked sarcastically, "I suppose it's all very grand." The Russian guide, Adams said, was pleased by Frost's response, for it confirmed the image of him as a man of the common people. I was very glad I hadn't been along.

Now that I think back on it, it seems a little joke that we had come into this city, still the symbol of all Russian elegance, on Monday the third, Labor Day. That same evening, in the Theater of the First Five-Year Plan Palace of Culture on Decembrists' Street, formerly Officers' Street, over the edge of the theatrical center of town, Shvarts's play *The Dragon* had its première. A satiric spoof of the Nazi system and of totalitarianism in general, it was put on by Akimov, director of the Theater of Comedy, the man who had introduced Shvarts's plays to Soviet audiences some twenty-five years before. But we weren't a theater-going group. One trip to the ballet had been enough. Never mind problems of language, our time was very short.

We dined with Daniil Granin, a novelist, who, like most of the successful people, had a town apartment and a small country dacha. Granin had achieved considerable notoriety with his 1955 *The Searchers*, one of the first post-Stalin novels to point up the discrepancies between the announced goals of Soviet life and the bourgeois, hypocritical practices of the entrenched bureaucrats. Nikolai Braun, the poet, and Alexander Popov, a well-known writer for younger readers, were there. So were Dar, Vera Panova, a widely respected novelist and short-story writer who had been in the United States with Simonov two years before, a young poet Sergei Orlov, and the movie director Kozintsev. Granin's wife and daughter were hostesses. Frost, Adams, Matlock, the two guides, and myself — it wasn't a small party. And, like many of our evenings, it wasn't an easy party. The hostess was worried about what Frost could or would eat, and the host was cautious about what could or would be said. For all the pleasant informality of dining "at home" and for all the care and extravagance with which the table was set, these evenings sometimes had a ceiling on them, an invisible partition which the conversation would lightly rise against and then fall back from into chatter and safe gossip. Perhaps the occasions were too official. Perhaps the presence of the Russian guides was an obvious restraint on candid conversation. Above all, I think, many of these writers felt far removed from Frost. They knew little, if any, of his work. Their notion of him as a solitary, metaphysical poet working in the craggy Vermont hills was remote from the obligations which they, as writers, felt and from the complicated political and literary worlds in which they had to live. To what extent politics played a role is hard to determine. But I found it surprising that here, among these very top Leningrad writers, nobody was really talking. Panova, a fine novelist, well read, hardly said a word. Frost talked at length about politics — the less his hosts said, the more he expatiated — but neither Granin nor the others replied except superficially, out of courtesy.

A few people said a poem or two. Braun politely declined, saying he never paid that much attention to his own work, especially at a dinner. Frost chuckled and agreed he didn't, either. Young Sergei Orlov was prevailed on to recite. Shortly afterwards the party broke up. It was a pleasant evening, but tame. It left you wondering where you really were. And I remember that, on the way back to the hotel, I suddenly wondered to myself if Ilya Ehrenburg were indeed unwell. We'd been told that he was at his dacha north of Moscow, that he wasn't well, and that he couldn't come into the city to see Frost and that he couldn't receive him in the country. Besides, we were told, our plans had been made. How could we change them now to go out to Ehrenburg? Very likely he was sick, but what you're *told*, just like that, so often isn't true that you quickly tend to believe nothing except what you yourself see. Frost, who had come to Russia expressly to talk poetry and politics, was getting weary of these well-intentioned but, as he thought, passive literary folk. On top of it all, after a night of no sleep and an afternoon of unhappy sight-seeing, he was tired. We tried to buoy him up by reminding him that tomorrow he'd meet Akhmatova and would give his first reading. He went to bed in a hinged frame of mind: things could easily swing either way.

TUESDAY

A tale of the road should have many digressions in it. Do you remember all the trips, physical and metaphysical, which

Sterne took on his way through France? Dunton and Rabelais were sidewinders, too. So were Gogol and Bulgakov. And so were we, in our sedate, well-publicized, mid-twentieth-century way.

Proposed trips to Khrushchev's birthplace and Tolstoy's burial place had been dropped in favor of evening talks and poetry readings. A number of times, though, Frost asked out loud, what the hell was he doing here? He hadn't come to make a survey of marinated mushrooms or caviar; he wasn't concerned with people's clothes — he never described that in his poems, either, he said — and what did all the wining and dining add up to? If he didn't see Khrushchev, would the trip be worthwhile? After all, he wasn't a State Department emissary. The Russians had invited him; he was their guest; but did they understand him? Would they understand a poetry reading? He had his own way of saying his poems and of talking. Would he get across? So far from New England and the audiences at home which he knew, he was unsure, and he worried that the expedition itself might seem to his friends and especially to the Russians a ridiculous imposition, a pretentious claim to an implausible universality cooked up by his publisher and by misguided well-wishers.

On the other hand, the side trips built up an impression in Frost's mind. The drives through the countryside and the evenings at home with people with whom he could easily joke gave him a sense of the personality of the country and of its

101

highest ability. Like the trip to Peredelkino, a few days before, and like the trip to Gagra, a few days later — the trip within the trip that confirmed the spectacular success of the entire adventure — the trip today north of Leningrad gave Frost a chance to see countryside he recognized as familiar and to talk to poets, people of his own style and frame of mind.

Adams was to be busy morning and afternoon with visits to the Hermitage in the Winter Palace and to the rare book department of the Leningrad Public Library. The rest of us, in a black Zim, followed by a Tass reporter in a Volga, drove out to Komarovo on the shore road along the Gulf of Finland. We had been invited to have lunch with Academician Mikhail Alexeyev, the outstanding Russian specialist on French and English literature and director of research at the Pushkin House, where Frost was to read his poems that evening.

From the Astoria we went down toward the Neva, around the Admiralty with its gilt, needle-like spire, past the Winter Palace and down to the Liteinyi Bridge onto the Petersburg side, out what is now Kirov Prospect to the mainland and left up along the shore past occasional sailboats at their moorings and parties of late-summer vacationers in the little resort towns north of the city. Some of the houses and public buildings show by their architecture that most of this ground was Finnish not long ago, though it has always been a popular Russian resort area. The soil is sandy. There are forests of tall pines. And the salt water is nearby.

Komarovo and its writers' and academicians' settlement are a five-minute walk from the beach, a fifty-minute drive from Leningrad. Alexeyev's dacha, with its waist-high wooden fence and carefully tended garden, is a simple, charming summer house. It is light and cheery, inside and out.

Alexeyev and his family greeted us. On the way, I had tried to explain to Frost whom we were going to see, where, and why, and had indicated that I believed Anna Akhmatova would be there, too, the finest living poet of Russia. I was excited. I felt deep respect and warm affection for these people, and I knew that dining in their company, plus a successful reading, would later mean more to Frost than any ballet or palace and, above all, would give him a picture to remember of a real Russia of which he had had no preconception. Because little Russian poetry has been translated into English — and even less translated interestingly — Frost had hardly any information about it at all. And the lists of Russian names were too tongue-twisting for him to keep straight. He had to go very much by face and by conversation. Which made our trip this day all the more important.

We, with our guides and our escort, arrived at the Alexeyevs' before noon. The day was sunny and cool. Alexeyev took Frost on a walk through his garden, proudly pointing out among the trees the small North American blue spruce that he had planted opposite the glassed-in sun porch and outside the dining room. We went inside and sat in Alexeyev's study, the Tass reporter on the sofa with open notebook on her knee. Frost and Alexeyev talked amiably about gardening and America and lunch and books, both somewhat taut, rather obviously discomfited that what they wished to be no more than pleasant social talk was being recorded for all the world to read as if it were a final judgment. The conversation kept halting at unseen stop signs, as if there were an infinite network of roads in the air and you could never be sure which one you actually were on.

Lunch was drawing near. Akhmatova arrived. She came in a dark dress, a pale lilac shawl over her shoulders, august and dignified with her white hair and deep eyes. She and Frost greeted each other with polite deference. At table Alexeyev toasted Frost and then toasted both Akhmatova and Frost, referring to their meeting as one of the great literary events of our time. The rumor was then pervasive that the two great poets were in competition for the Nobel Prize. They themselves were conscious of the stakes, the rumors, and the pressures, but neither one let on. Later, they said they knew what they were up against, but at the time only tension expressed awareness of the competition — tension and Frost's increased desire to confront Khrushchev.

We sat around the table in the sun-filled dining room, the lunch a seven-course dinner, the conversation turning to both American and English writers and to the Greek and Latin classics, topics on which Akhmatova, Frost, and Alexeyev were all extremely well read. Akhmatova, Frost, and Alexeyev, some twenty years younger than the other two, were people intellectually of the same generation. Akhmatova and Frost both had begun to be recognized poets just before the First World War. They both had had long and exceptional careers, bringing them, in their different ways, to the same point: each was the leading poet of his country, of a whole national literary culture and tradition. Here they were, sitting at lunch, symbols, so we thought, of the reunion of that understanding which almost a hundred years earlier had existed between Turgenev and James and which seemed to us all, despite the absence of any "profound" discussion, more important than the parleys of politicians.

Frost seemed to feel out of things. Possibly he was only very nervous about his reading that evening. At any rate, after several Russians had much praised Akhmatova, I put in some highly praiseful phrases about Frost. He snapped out angrily, "No more of that, none of that, you cut that out." I nodded, started to try to explain what I had meant, but he refused to listen. "Cut it out," he repeated.

Pressed to say a poem, he declined, immediately deferring to Akhmatova. An Italian recording of some of her poems was played, and then she recited two short, recent poems. She sat in an armchair by the window in the light-filled, cream-colored living room. Her shawl was still over her shoulders. Her hands lay in her lap. She recited:

> *My own I won't weep over,*
> *But I'd rather not ever see*
> *The golden brand of failure*
> *On a brow still calm and serene.*

And then she said, in her soft but emotionally strong and expressive voice, a poem which refers to four powerful, passionate women from the world's history who directed their passion to serve the integrity of the nation in which they had transcendent faith. She had written the poem just six days before, she said, the very day that Frost had arrived in Russia, though then she hadn't known about that.

> *"The Last Rose"*
> > You will write about us obliquely.
> > —I.B.

> *I bend my head when Morozova bows in prayer;*
> *I dance with Herod's stepdaughter Salomé;*
> *I fly up on the smoke from Dido's fire*
> *to be with Joan again at her auto-da-fé.*
>
> *O Lord! You see, I am too tired to be*
> *resurrected more, or made to die, or live.*
> *Take everything away, but let me feel*
> *anew the freshness of this bright red rose.*

"You translate it," she said to me, as soon as she had finished, but I said I couldn't, just like that, and paraphrased it for Frost.

"It's very musical," he said, "you can hear the music in it." He smiled and nodded, "It's very good, it sounds very good." He was being polite, was saying what he sensed was expected of him, and he had been moved by the poet's voice and by her expression. He knew she had authority, but he couldn't reach its source, and I felt that he couldn't know in what sense the history of Russian literature seemed suddenly focused in a moment by the poem's last line. He felt very foreign again, unable to know how, in Russian, too, nothing is more exigent than the reality of a beautiful thing. He could sense that the others felt something special, but he couldn't touch it himself.

Hearing Akhmatova herself recite the poem moved us all. The whole group was so caught by the immediacy of the poem and by the life and understanding which it represented that for a few seconds we were silent, still. The incommunicability of the poem's substance had fallen like a shadow over the room. Frost remembered this, and he remembered Akhmatova's expression, for he commented later how grand she was but how sad she seemed to be.

We'd had tea and coffee. Alexeyev, his wife and daughter said good-by, waved cheerfully, and reminded us we'd meet again in the Pushkin House at six. Frost had to rest first and to have time with himself before the reading. He always did.

The Pushkin House stands on Vasily Island across the Neva from the Winter Palace. It's not far from what used to be the Stock Exchange. We went through the dark, stone-floored lobby, up the wide marble stairs, down the corridor and into Alexeyev's office. We opened the leather-padded door, pushed the portière aside, and found ourselves in an office much as it must have been years ago. The grandfather clock in the corner said "London 1804" on the moon of its face. Alexeyev, Bushmin the director of the Pushkin House, Stepanov the librarian — Frost met one distinguished scholar after another, including the younger Shakespeare specialist Levin.

The auditorium of the museum was packed. A baize-covered table had been set up at one end, in between marble columns. There was a big vase of flowers on it and several chairs, in rows, behind it. To the left, as you faced it, was a lectern. In back of you, to one side of the room, was a television camera. Cables and wires ran along the parquet floor. Back of the green baize-covered table, the floor was a jungle of wires and coils. Nikolai Braun presided at the reading, and Alexeyev also spoke, both men praising Frost for his poetry, thanking him for honoring Leningrad and the Pushkin House with a visit, and expressing their own delight at having him and having been brought literally in touch with contemporary American writers and writing. Frost joked with his audience, much in the style he used at home, and we were surprised at the audience's quick response: they understood, and they laughed with him.

Frost read some of his best-known poems, followed by young Leningrad poets reading translations they had made, not always of the same poems. No matter. Frost read "Two Tramps in Mud Time," "Birches," "Mending Wall," "The Road Not Taken," "The Gift Outright," "Spring Pools," "The Pasture," "The Cabin in the Clearing," "Away," "Departmental." Every so often the television lights would come up brightly into our eyes as we sat behind that baize-covered table and the camera would grind. Frost would keep on "saying" his poems and interpolating his comments. Afterwards, as the half-hour biographical film was being shown and we stood in Alexeyev's office, crowded with well-wishers, Frost indicated his pleased surprise at how well the reading had gone, at how well he had been understood. For a moment, I think, he felt pleased with himself: he had made good on foreign ground in a world of readers he hadn't expected to find. He was glad to have met Akhmatova that afternoon but discouraged by the impossibility of communicating as he would have liked to. After the reading that evening, he felt sportive, damned if he was going to bounce around sleeplessly on a train again, and almost ready to forget altogether about seeing Khrushchev.

We dined in the hotel, Braun and Popov with us. Then most of the group vanished in the black Zim to the Red Arrow back to Moscow, while Frost and I stayed on to catch a plane in the morning. We talked about the visible and invisible changes in the city the last hundred years, about the permanence of poetry and the impermanence of politics, for all its power, and he made little jokes and puns on Aristotle's definition that the good is that at which all things aim. I don't remember how he put it, but he said you often have to approach the good backward, or come up from the back side; some people shoot it because they don't know what to do with it, just take aim, but that doesn't change anything at all. "It's all how well you play the game," he said, "can you really do it or not. That's the great thing about Khrushchev," he said, "he did it, he just went right in, he's not afraid of power. He knows what power is, and he's not afraid of it. That's what you've got to do."

Suddenly he was tired and ready for bed. The flush of the evening had worn off, I suspect, and our talk had unexpectedly brought up to the surface of his mind the unfulfilled desire which he had been trying to repress. His mind was off poetry again and back on the political world of Moscow.

WEDNESDAY

The Russians joke that you go between Moscow and Leningrad so fast that you can't even smoke a cigarette. It's not quite true, of course, but it is true that there's little time between the moment when the NO SMOKING light goes off at the end of the jet plane's climb and the moment when it goes back on at the start of its descent. Suddenly in mid-morning we were in Moscow.

A cluster of friends and escorts met Frost at Vnukovo Airport. Among them was a young university graduate student from Odessa, Valentina Kuznetsova, who had come up to interview Frost. She was writing her dissertation on Frost, the man she regarded as the greatest Western poet. It was, for him, a special tribute. This young woman's informed enthusiasm indicated the affectionate respect which the Russians felt for him. To her delight, Frost granted her a long interview as soon as we were back in our hotel. And he told us at lunch afterwards that he had been impressed by the young woman's good knowledge of American poetry, including his own, and by her intelligent questions.

A second public reading was scheduled for the evening, so after our late lunch, Adams and I left Frost to rest. Adams went to see some rare books at the Lenin Library, and I went to buy some books down on Blacksmith Bridge, a street famous in the eighteenth century for fine shops and now well-known for bookstores, a café, and a sporting-goods store. When we returned, our poet friend, we found out, had put his overcoat on and gone for a walk down the avenue. Just like that. He had a sparkle in his eye and an urchin-like grin at having so neatly "tricked" us. It was another way of proving, if only for a moment, that here in Russia, too, he wasn't dependent on anybody.

INVITATION

The USSR Writers Union and
The All-Union Library of Foreign Literature
invite you to attend
an evening
with the most outstanding American
poet

ROBERT FROST

under the chairmanship of A. Surkov.

Robert Frost will read from his poems.

R. Frost's poems
in Russian translation will be read by
M. Zenkevich, I. Kashkin, A. Sergeyev.
There will be a showing of

an American film about Robert Frost
in color.
The evening will take place
5 September 1962
in the Auditorium of the
All-Union Library of Foreign Literature
12 Razin Street, Third Floor
Tel: B-1-08-79
at 7 p.m.

A few days later, when asked what he thought of the climate for writers in Russia, Frost said, "It looks very salubrious, a very good climate for artists. I saw the model for the new library of modern languages — a beautiful building. Nothing more magnificent could be going on in favor of the arts."

Surkov introduced Frost to an audience of about seven hundred. People were standing in the halls and corridors. It was clear at once that Frost, who had "warmed up" in Leningrad the day before, felt confident, and that his audience was with him from the first. He said he was glad to be there, to have come over to see Russia and talk about poetry and politics, though "they're different things," he said. "Our two countries, mine and yours," he told the audience, "are great nations, and it's the duty of great nations to compete and see who's going to produce the greatest ruler. We won't call them kings any more. You can always tell a great ruler if he's a great dreamer," Frost added, "if he's got a lot of the dreamer in him." He paused a moment. "And we won't name any names." The audience was very unsure of Frost's meaning; you could see it shift nervously. "That was an extemporaneous poem," Frost said, saving the situation, "free verse." Everyone laughed.

"Leningrad is still a royal city, it has lingering royalism," said Frost, announcing he had just returned from there. "Moscow is a proletarian city, or if you don't like that word too well, if it's worn out with you, then I'll call it a people's city," and he smiled. His audience again easily understood his words but not the attitude which they expressed. It didn't know how to respond. "You have lots of things going on here," he said, "all the books of poetry being published and the new library they showed me. You're doing a lot for the arts." His admiration was genuine, though he would have chosen a political way different than the Russian. He had his audience back with him again. At several moments on the trip I thought that now, in his old age, he would have been pleased to have been a court poet, but even in imagination I couldn't pick a court that would do.

Frost was egged on enough by the rapport with his audience to begin reciting his poems from memory, to recite from memory passages from the poems he was reading. He read many of his most popular, shorter poems, trying always to adjust his selection to what had been translated. "Mending Wall," which he had read the night before, had been one of the first to be translated in the late 1930's, and Frost read it that evening as a poem he knew audiences always asked for, not as a commentary on Berlin, which one reporter unfortunately interpreted it to be.

The great difference between the average American's — or the average American reporter's — antagonism to Russia and Frost's "needling" of his hosts lay in Frost's genuine respect for Russian power. He liked it. He liked to see men handling life. As in his quarrel with the church, he was all on God and the Devil's side and fed up with the clerical preachers of virtue.

Surkov closed the evening, after some translations had been read, by saying, "I know that Mr. Frost is a personal friend of President Kennedy, and I'd like to ask Mr. Frost to pass on to his President a request that he send more just such ambassadors [as Frost] to the Soviet Union."

A number of people were standing around outside on the street. Frost asked what they were doing there and Adams said they were waiting for him. Frost went back toward them, waved to them and gave them greetings and thanks. They cheered and waved, and we set off for our hotel.

After the reading, Adams had learned from a reporter — and Matlock, whom we now talked to, confirmed it — that Secretary Udall was leaving the next morning for Gagra to see Premier Khrushchev. We tried to find out if anything could be done to have Frost invited also, but though arrangements for a visit by Frost were still being pressed, nothing seemed to be forthcoming. Frost didn't even know that Udall was back in Moscow. We knew that Frost would be piqued, would feel deceived, would raise hell and curse us all out if Udall went down and he didn't. We decided to say nothing that night, in case we could reach Udall before the plane left the next morning, before the scheduled taping of the television show. Ironically, the conversation in Frost's room after dinner turned on precisely the topic of a meeting with Khrushchev.

From the start of the trip in Washington, Frost had repeatedly talked about seeing Khrushchev, about getting across not only his notion of the roles of courage and excellence in contemporary politics but also of persuading the Russian premier to take a stand for greatness, to cut through political entanglements and to lay bare the "noble rivalry" which, Frost believed, must be the destiny of the United States and the Soviet Union. Sitting in his hotel room this September evening, in an armchair by a TV set that he never turned on, he told Adams and me that he wanted to tell Khrushchev to stop allowing nations to haggle, to deliver East Berlin to West Berlin, to guarantee something like the Polish Corridor, and to put an end to the whole argument. "If there's going to be a fight," he said he wanted to tell him, "if there has to be a fight, let it be over something really big." Khrushchev, he repeated, was a great leader, a man who wasn't afraid of power. Frost counted on getting to him and on being understood by him.

THURSDAY

Just after dawn on Thursday, Matlock raced out to the airport but missed the Udall plane. There was now no help for it: we had to tell Frost.

Breakfast nearly over, the television recording still more than two hours away, Adams broke the news to him. When he heard about it, he was annoyed. He said that all his friends were running out on him. We tried to assure him that Udall had surely had to go on his own business and that maybe he was arranging Frost's visit, too. Adams stepped out of the room a moment to talk to a reporter about the allegedly political reading of "Mending Wall" the night before. I tried to remind Frost what a success he had made, how his trip was a literary triumph. I could get nowhere. With a wave of his hand, as if to say we were all damned liars and no-goods (he regularly twitted translators about cheating on him), he refused to talk about anything. I went out. Adams went in but soon came back, saying that Frost had turned on him sharply: "Don't you preach to me, Fred Adams." In half an hour or so, Frost would be on the air before the cameras. Now he was alone and angry. We had no idea what to do.

Upstairs, not much after eleven, Frost, Surkov and Yevtushenko, one of the guides and myself between them, the three Russian poet-translators at another table at one side, sat in front of the television cameras. Tests for volume, lighting were made. Cigarettes were put out. Adams, Matlock and myself were ready for a bomb. Surkov introduced Frost briefly, and Frost immediately thanked his Russian hosts for the good time they had given him, for the dinners in their houses and the responsive poetry readings. He acknowledged the literary "theme" of his trip and responded to his hosts' cordiality. We felt that he had triumphed.

Surkov asked how Frost would define poetry in the life of

a nation. Frost said that it was like women: it was not a direct power, but it exerted a powerful influence. Yevtushenko, Adams noted down, asked, "Some poets have a tendency to slight the importance of labor, to say that the soul is everything. Don't you think a man's soul is found in working?"

"Yes," said Frost, Adams recorded, "in the labor of his hands. My three kinds are mowing with a scythe, chopping with an ax, and writing with a pen. I pity the people who don't know the world from working in it, who just go around kicking up the dirt. Most of my figures of speech are from farming, and sometimes a few from games. A poem I'll say in a minute, 'The Tuft of Flowers,' was written sixty years and more ago, and it's about my boyhood days when I worked on farms. It tells what my brand of socialism was then, and it's my brand now." And he said the poem that ends:

> *"Men work together," I told him from the heart,*
> *"Whether they work together or apart."*

After the show, Frost shook hands with Surkov and Yevtushenko and the technicians in a gesture of friendship and magnanimity. For a few minutes, Mr. K. was off his mind.

We went down to Frost's room. Yevtushenko came in. We sat at the round table in the center. Yevtushenko was more than friendly. He sat with his back to the window next to Frost, leaned forward on the table, and lit a cigarette. There was no talk of labor and poetry and the workers of the world.

Yevtushenko seemed sincere, simple, inquisitive, eager to please. In Paris, several months later, he declared that there were no "isms" for him, only good and bad art, and that Whitman and Frost were among the poets he most admired. Here, in the hotel room, he seemed anxious to discover the correctness of his taste and to know the style of excellence properly to be adopted. Upstairs, in front of the public cameras, he had talked on acceptable public topics. In the room, now, he relaxed. He wanted a "poet-to-poet" talk. He seemed to want Frost to like him, to understand him and to respect him. He turned abruptly to Frost, complaining about damage done to Russian artists by a previous *Life* magazine article on abstract art in Russia. He asked whom Frost considered the best modern American artist.

Frost paused a moment, put off, it seemed, by Yevtushenko's obvious earnestness. "Well," he said, "there's my friend Andy Wyeth." There was another pause. Yevtushenko was clearly extremely disappointed, and yet confused. He hadn't expected that answer — neither had I — but he was unsure what to make of it. He respected Frost's seniority — it seemed to me that Frost represented a sort of iconoclastic standard and individualistic senior poet image which Yevtushenko craved — and he admired Frost's culture. In this brief chat at table, Yevtushenko was both polite and modest. There was none of his public brashness and flamboyance. Yet what could he make of himself, you felt, if he weren't publicly flamboyant? Even here, the answer to his question a failure, everything seemed stacked against him.

Lunch that day was a formal affair at the American Embassy. The new ambassador had not yet arrived; the chargé d'affaires, McSweeney, was host. A handful of Russians had been invited, along with ourselves. Tvardovsky was unable to come because of illness. But Surkov came, and Simonov, and Valentin Katayev, who later visited Frost in the hospital in Boston, and Georgii Markov, who moved into a position of power in the Writers Union following the antiliberal crackdown later that winter. Everybody was courteous, cool and deferential, ate nuts and sipped cocktails, and said the carefully correct thing at table. It was very much a formal lunch in every sense, with American food and American furniture, in the heart of Moscow. The best thing that came of it was a proposal by Mrs. McSweeney to take Frost shopping to buy presents for his family — a shopping trip that had to be put off another day. For suddenly the next morning we found ourselves flying to Gagra.

FRIDAY

The mountains of the Caucasus lay beneath us like brown fishbacks on an azure sea. We were flying at 10,000 feet. The whole world was bright. Down in the olive-dark valleys there were roads and rivers, lying like twisted wisps of thread on a dark carpet. You could see houses and long barns and fields.

We were a planeload of vacationers, or pale city people headed for three weeks of watermelons and sun. Except four of us. Four of us were vacationers of a kind, all right, but we weren't coming for watermelons and sun. Besides me, we were Frost, Surkov, and Anatoly Myshkov, an able translator from the American Desk of the Soviet Foreign Office.

Frost had dozed intermittently during the flight. The plane had hummed along vibrating soporifically as machines do, and Frost had kept napping. The others talked.

Ever since the end of July when President Kennedy had formally asked Frost to make this Russian trip, the poet had thought of the role he would play. To the President's request to represent the United States in this cultural exchange, Frost had replied by letter on July 24:

DEAR MR. PRESIDENT:

How grand of you to think of me this way and how like you to take the chance of sending anyone like me over there affinatizing with the Russians. You must know a lot about me besides my rank from my poems but think how the professors interpret the poems! I am almost as full of politics and history as you are. I like to tell the story of the mere sailor-boy from upstate New York who by favor of his captain and the American consul at St. Petersburg got to see the Czar in St. Petersburg with the gift in his hand of an acorn that fell from a tree that stood by the house of George Washington. That was in the 1830's when proud young Americans were equal to anything. He said to the Czar, "Washington was a great ruler and you're a great ruler and I thought you might like to plant the acorn with me by your palace." And so he did. I have been having a lot of historic parallels lately: a big one between Caesar's imperial democracy that made so many millions equal under arbitrary power and the Russian democracy. Ours is a more Senatorial democracy like the Republic of Rome. I have thought I saw the Russian and American democracies drawing together, theirs easing down from a kind of abstract severity to taking less and less care of the masses: ours creeping up to taking more and more care of the masses as they grew innumerable. I see us becoming the two great powers of the modern world in noble rivalry while a third power of United Germany, France, and Italy, the common market, looks on as an expanded polyglot Switzerland.

I shall be reading poems chiefly, over there, but I shall be talking some where I read and you may be sure I won't be talking just literature. I'm the kind of democrat that *will* reason. You know my admiration for your "Profiles." I am frightened by this big undertaking but I was more frightened at your Inauguration. I am glad Stewart [Udall] will be along to take care of me. He has been a good influence in my life. And Fred[erick] Adams of the Morgan Library. I had a very good talk with Anatoly Dobrynin in Washington last May. You probably know that my Adams House at Harvard has an oil portrait of one of our old boys, Jack Reed [John Reed, the newspaper reporter and author of *Ten Days that Shook the World,* who is buried in the Kremlin wall], which nobody has succeeded in making us take down.

Forgive the long letter. I don't write letters but you have stirred my imagination and I have been interested in Russia as a power ever since Rurik came to Novgorod; and these are my credentials. I could go on with them like this to make the picture complete: about the English-speaking world of England, Ireland, Canada, and Australia, New Zealand and Us versus the Russian-speaking world for the next century or so, mostly a stand-off but now and then a showdown to test our mettle. The rest of the world would be Asia and Africa, more or less negligible for the time being, though it needn't be too openly declared. Much of this would be the better for not being declared openly but kept always in the back of our minds in all our diplomatic and other relations. I am describing not so much what ought to be but what is and will be — reporting and prophesying. This is the way we are one world, as you put it, of independent nations interdependent — the separateness of the parts as important as the connection of the parts.

Great times to be alive, aren't they?

> Sincerely yours,
> ROBERT FROST

Frost's eminence at eighty-eight allowed him the privilege of assuming a simplicity that was not naturally his. It also constrained him to require of himself and his intelligence a solution, or the formulation of a "problem," in dramatically simple, but profound terms. He wasn't pretending to be a sailor, but he felt he represented his people. He was going to see the chief political officer of the Soviet Union — the other great country in the world, Frost often said — and he would have liked to have proposed a gesture as simple and as meaningful as the sailor boy's. Nevertheless, for all his repetition of the sailor boy's story and for all his talk of a horse trade with the Russians, he himself was aware that the world *had* changed since the 1830's, since his own boyhood in the 1880's, even since his first popular success in the 1920's, and he was unsure that the political role he would have liked to play was playable at all. Still, he said, he was going to tell them, tell the Russians, what he meant — but he half-doubted that they would understand.

In fact, what he didn't think he could get across to them, he did: they sensed his poetic talent, his deep humanity, his wit and independence. What he hoped he could persuade them to accept, they rejected: they disapproved of his political analyses and proposals. But even as the Russians rejected Frost's politics, they admired his tenacity and quick-witted arguments. They respected him for believing what they neither could nor would. And he, for his part, admired them for establishing precisely what he had argued against all his life: socialist democracy. "We're laid out for rivalry in sports, science, art and democracy," Frost said, "by courtesy we call them both democracies." By democracy he meant, he said, "a more earnest desire than the world has ever had before to take care of everybody." He didn't like it, he would always add, but that was the way the world was going — and maybe it was even a good thing. The course of civilization, he said, as he had written in "Kitty Hawk," was west northwest:

> *Then for years and years*
> *And for miles and miles*
> *'Cross the Aegean Isles,*
> *Athens Rome France Britain,*
> *Always West Northwest,*
> *As have I not written,*
> *Till the so-long kept*
> *Purpose was expressed*
> *In the leap we leapt.*
> *And the radio*
> *Cried, "The Leap — the Leap!"*
> *It belonged to US,*
> *Not to our friends the Russ. . . .*

Political activity he characterized as "a vaulting match . . . [with] ourselves — mankind, in a love and hate rivalry combine." Progress, social betterment, the welfare of society — he was

skeptical of the worth of do-gooders, or the activists, of re-
formers:

> *Someone says the Lord*
> *Says our reaching toward*
> *Is its own reward.*
> *One would like to know*
> *Where God says it though.*

Having endured indifference and failure until nearly forty,
he could not help wanting popular affection, but he could
never believe in it, and he never felt sure that he had it. He
didn't accept the myth of himself which he had created.

On Thursday, the evening before, we had dined at the
Matlocks'. Frost with pleasure ate American food and joked
with the Matlocks' small children. Then the invitation came
through. Matlock answered a phone call and returned beam-
ing — Frost was invited to visit Khrushchev the next day. He
would leave Moscow on a jet flight at eight in the morning.

We went back to the hotel around ten-thirty. On the way,
Frost suddenly said he felt wobbly, unwell. Adams, an old and
cherished friend, lightly teased and coddled him. Perhaps it
was passing indigestion.

Back in his room, Frost swallowed some stomach stiff-
ener, which he didn't like at all. He continued to feel worse.
We talked to him about alternatives, about what he would
think of himself afterwards if he didn't go. We persuaded him

to decide nothing until the morning. He was to leave the hotel at six-thirty. We'd be in at a quarter to six, we said; there would be some breakfast at six. Then we could decide everything. We said good-night, and he shut his door. He didn't like you "to do" for him, though when he wanted something he had to have it right away.

Outside in the corridor, Adams and I talked a while longer. He knew some of Frost's previous illnesses and Frost's special ways. We both agreed that Frost was, above all, suddenly extremely nervous. For we knew how he prepared himself for a poetry reading, how he would spend an hour or two by himself in his room beforehand, and how he would dine only afterward. The impending trip was no mere reading. And he was so deeply committed to his poetic-prophetic-political role that, of course, he had to be nervous. But if he was, also, sick? If he were to get sicker? We agreed to decide everything in the morning—or, really, by daylight, for by now it was almost dawn.

Adams's alarm clock rang. He woke me. We dressed, went to Frost. He said he was worse but would go to Gagra. "That's what I came for," he said. Adams and I asked Frost which of us he wanted along, for only one companion was included in the Premier's invitation. Frost joked about Freddy's Russian and absolutely needing me. "We're in this all together, aren't we?" he said. And we all agreed we were indeed. By six-thirty we were downstairs ready to meet Surkov. By eight-fifteen we were in the air.

At ten-fifty we were at the airport outside Sochi. A delegation met us, the same government officials and engineers who had greeted Udall the day before, and escorted us to a waiting limousine, a black Chaika with curtains around the windows and a chauffeur who drove as fast as hell, one hand on the horn. An hour later we had crossed the border into Georgia and driven up to the Guest House of the Georgian SSR Ministry of Health. We were to wash, rest, eat a little, and then drive another twenty minutes to the Prime Minister's dacha.

A dining room and lounge were downstairs. Frost's and my room was on the second floor. A balcony outside overlooked a lush subtropical garden of palms, bananas, orange and lemon trees. The sea lay beyond, azure and beautiful in the yellow southern light.

Frost felt worse. He lay down. He napped. He complained his stomach hurt more. No, he didn't want anything to eat or drink, just some "perry," he said, meaning the pear-flavored soda he had taken a liking to.

The rest of us in the group sat down to lunch in the dining room, somewhat confused. Our hosts were upset; Surkov and Myshkov were somewhat incredulous and much concerned; I was as nervous as Frost. I kept leaving the table and looking in on him. The second time that I asked if he wanted a doctor, he said yes.

The host at the guest house came in. We took Frost's temperature. Frost said he couldn't go any farther. I said we'd better call a doctor. Twenty minutes later a young girl (most doctors in Russia are women) came walking up the hill. She wore a white frock and carried her little doctor's bag. She checked Frost's temperature, took his pulse, listened to his chest and back, suggested he drink some soup or tea, agreed that he wasn't very well but that he didn't seem really sick. It seemed, she said, to be a case of indigestion and probably the strain of so much traveling. She agreed that if it was something serious, he ought to be in Moscow. Frost kept saying he couldn't go any farther, he just couldn't.

I told Surkov that Frost couldn't travel any farther, that he was done in. I went back to Frost and the doctor, who stayed with him the whole time and even saw him to the plane. Surkov got on the phone. Fifteen minutes later he came back and said that the Premier was sending his own doctor over and would soon follow himself. Khrushchev had made the gesture of a master. When I told Frost what would happen, he was obviously relieved — and yet, also, even more nervous, for the meeting was imminent.

Time passed. Frost dozed. The rest of us in our shirtsleeves stood out on the balcony overlooking the sea, talking, saying how we would like to stay on and go swimming there. The young doctor sat downstairs by herself and kept coming up to check on Frost. I looked in every few minutes.

Surkov pleaded business and disappeared, Myshkov with him. I kept walking up and down along the balcony. For what seemed a long time there was nobody around. Just the palms and the sea, the stucco walls, and Frost, dozing.

I was in the room when suddenly Khrushchev's doctor came in. He was a sun-tanned, attractive man, slim, middle-aged, with glasses, in a tan nankeen jacket. He was all business. He examined Frost very carefully, just as the other doctor had done, but with the authority that comes of confidence and position. As he examined Frost, he asked me for Frost's medical history, how long we had traveled. I answered as best I could, citing Frost's previous internal disorder, stating when we had arrived, and insisting that, for a number of reasons, we had to get back to Moscow that night. Frankly, I didn't think Frost could stand being isolated in this resort town. The doctor kept nodding significantly and suggesting that Frost was just worn out. His temperature was 101.5 degrees.

The doctor rose, recommended diet and rest, and left the room. I told Frost that Khrushchev would come soon.

Everything was quiet again. The palm leaves outside the windows rose and fell slowly like broad fans. Frost shut his eyes. I started to read a book but couldn't concentrate for as much as a sentence. The sand-colored linen slipcovers on the chairs seemed suddenly to say not that it was summertime but that we had fallen into the wrong room, the wrong world — that we weren't guests but an accident. Minutes of waiting stretched out like days. I kept going out into the hall to check the clock.

Nobody came. Nothing happened. I went out to see if indeed the Premier had come. I noticed a man out front, and called to him. He stared hard at me, said he knew nothing, and disappeared inside. He didn't come back. With a strange uneasiness, as if in a haunted castle, though it was bright and sunny everywhere, I went back in and out onto the balcony. Where had everybody gone?

I turned a corner on the balcony and suddenly saw, sitting at the table where, an hour before, Surkov, Myshkov and I had been making small talk, Khrushchev and Surkov in discussion.

Our time was getting shorter and shorter, and Frost was getting worse waiting. A moment later Surkov presented me to the Premier. I said Frost was not well, was very grateful to have had the doctor, extremely pleased that the Premier had come to the guest house, and very anxious to see him. Khrushchev's doctor appeared and Khrushchev asked him for a diagnosis. The doctor gave a detailed authentic account. Khrushchev summed it up by asking whether it meant he could see Frost or not. The doctor said he could. Khrushchev said, "Let's go."

When I told Frost that the Premier was coming, he swung himself up onto the edge of his bed. He put socks and shoes on. The Russians came in. We moved some chairs over. Khrushchev sat on one, right beside Frost. Myshkov sat on Frost's bed, translating Frost into Russian. I sat on the opposite bed, translating Khrushchev into English. Surkov sat on a chair at the foot of one bed; Lebedev, the Premier's secretary, sat on a chair at the foot of the other. The host of the guest house sat in another chair. The door and windows were open, and you could see the blue water in the distance.

Frost wore shirt and trousers. Khrushchev wore a natty summer suit, olive-tan in color, over a pale beige Ukrainian blouse. He was sun-tanned and healthy-looking, full of vigor and extremely courteous. He asked about Frost's health, chided him for not taking care of himself, expressed admiration at Frost's traveling so far, said how pleased he was to see him, reminded him to be sure to follow the doctor's orders if he was going to live to be a hundred. Frost, for his part, said that he was very glad to have come, that he was very pleased by the invitation, that you could never trust doctors anyway, and that he was certainly going to live to be a hundred because in the year he would be a hundred his country would be two hundred. It was something, he said, being half as old as your country.

Khrushchev asked him how he had found his stay in Russia, how he had been received. Frost replied that he had had a fine time, that the Premier certainly had done a lot for poetry, judging by all the poems that were published by all the poets around. They talked briefly about art and poetry and the artist's relation to society. Frost conveyed the President's greetings to the Premier and expressed his gratitude to those who had arranged his trip.

And with that the real conversation began. Khrushchev

wondered if Frost had anything special in his mind, and Frost started talking about what had long lain closest to his heart: a way for working out an East-West understanding.

He didn't talk down coexistence, as some of his Republican friends wanted him to. He made it clear from the first that he assumed the Soviet system was here to stay; that, like it or not, socialism was inevitable; and that he admired Premier Khrushchev for the audacity and courage with which he used power. Frost didn't doubt coexistence — though he never used the word; he referred to "rivalry" — but he did worry about the moral quality of the leaders of both sides and, therefore, about the permanence of their accomplishments. For he believed, some time before his Russian trip, that the morality of politicians determined their historical merit. He seriously meant that the 1960 Presidential election was symptomatic of an Augustan revival. The vigor of the age, he felt, promised a brilliant future.

He believed that the top thing a government could bestow was character. This was the poet's role in government. He repeated to Khrushchev what he had often said: a great nation makes great poetry, and great poetry makes a great nation. He had in mind just such a concept of political and intellectual grandeur when he told reporters the next day that his talk with Premier Khrushchev "was not on a low level of partisanship, [was] all high level." He was thinking of this when he told the Premier that there should be no petty squabbles, that there must be a noble rivalry between Russia and the United States, forcefully and magnanimously pressed by the leaders of both sides. "At our level," said Frost to Khrushchev, "there must be candid understanding."

Frost talked briefly about cultural exchange, said that it was a good thing but that it didn't go very far, didn't amount to much. And besides, he added, that's not where the real power is anyway. "We're laid out for rivalry in sports, science, art, democracy," he said. "That's the real test, which democracy's going to win?"

And the talk moved into the tense world of international politics and national prestige. The more Frost tried to bear down on his "modest proposals" for effecting a Berlin solution in the light of his own notion of political magnanimity, the more Khrushchev pointed out the hard reasoning supporting his own convictions. In response to Frost's suggestion of reuniting the two halves of Berlin, the Premier castigated the military organization of NATO, the recrudescence of Nazi power in West Germany, and the irresponsible politics of the Western Allies in allowing Germany to become a threat to peace once more. Frost said Germany wouldn't be a threat if united and demilitarized and given a commercial trade route. Khrushchev said Germany wasn't a threat actually anyway, any more than NATO was, because Soviet rockets could blast all Europe to smithereens in less than thirty minutes. If you really want to do something to regularize the situation, the Premier proposed, sign a peace treaty. That, he said, was what had happened in Austria, and look how stable the situation was there. The Premier told Frost that President Kennedy himself had said he wanted to sign a peace treaty but couldn't because of conditions, because of conditions at home. Frost reasserted his abhorrence of the possibility that bickering over Berlin — over what he considered basically an irrelevant issue — might provoke a huge war between the two giants of the world, the two countries to whom, he said, the next hundred years belong. The Premier said that the Warsaw Pact countries were forging ahead economically and that they would soon overtake the Common Market. And Frost came back to his theme of horse-trading, of recognizing the present limits of political power and the continual drawing closer of the capitalist and the planned economies, of what he called the democracy straining upward toward socialism and the socialist democracy humanizing downward from the severity of its ideal.

When pressed on Berlin, the Premier said that the West had no proper claim to East Berlin at all, that it was theirs. "There's nothing to trade," he said. He in turn proposed that Frost ask his President and his countrymen once more to consider establishing Berlin as a free city, garrisoned by UN troops, with (under these conditions) boundaries and access guaranteed by the Russians.

There was no doubt that both men were confident of the spirit of their countries and of the military power behind each.

Each man indicated that he and his country were willing to compete with the other. Frost said that, if there had to be a fight, it should be a big one, a basic one. But he advocated rivalry in everything else, in sports, business, arts — a rivalry which, he said, God wanted. "God wants us to contend," he said; "you have progress only in conflict." Premier Khrushchev said that the fundamental conflict between the two countries was peaceful economic competition. He said that the Soviet Union and all the Warsaw Pact nations were young countries, healthy, vital, full of energy. He said that they had made extraordinary strides forward. The United States and Western Europe, he said, were thousands of years old with a defunct economic system. This reminded him, he said, of an anecdote reported in Gorky's memoirs of Tolstoy, where Tolstoy told about being too old and too weak and too infirm to do it but still having the desire. Frost chuckled and said that might be true for the two of them but that the United States was too young to worry about that yet. Frost said that the Premier had great power and could do great good by effecting a political settlement through dealing unilaterally with the United States; that all Khrushchev had to do was to make a simple solution to the Berlin crisis and that the United States would accept it. "You have the soul of a poet," Premier Khrushchev replied.

Frost insisted on a distinction between European civilization on the one hand, and Asian and African on the other. To his impassioned plea for recognition of common European cultural values, shared by Russia and the United States, too, in contradistinction to what he called the absence of culture in Africa and the impossible foreignness of China, the Premier was restrained. He was patient. He had talked about the weakened American dollar and about the realignment of military power as the result of rockets — the oceans had virtually dried up, he said, and in the same way that the British Navy had vanished as a force, so the United States couldn't count on protection by isolation. The Russians were grateful to the Americans for many things, the Premier said, and reported how, the day before, he had joked with Secretary Udall, who had commended the Russians' extensive hydroelectric installations, that they had learned the techniques from Americans in the 1930s.

Frost kept coming back to political questions. In relations between the two countries, he said, there should be no blackguarding, no dirty play. There should be no more propaganda and no more name calling. This had to be stopped. And Khrushchev emphatically agreed.

He asked Frost if he weren't tired, if he, Khrushchev, hadn't overstayed his time. Frost said no, he was glad to have had such a frank, such a high-minded talk. Khrushchev asked Frost to be sure to give his greetings to the President and to the American people and to urge on the President consideration of the issues as Frost and Khrushchev had discussed them. "It is a great pleasure to have met such a famous poet," said the

Premier. He was glad that Frost was pleased by his trip to Russia, and he wished him a continued and completely successful creative career.

They were standing, shaking hands. Frost once more expressed his pleasure that the meeting had been arranged. Khrushchev turned politely, walked around the bed, and went out of the room. The others followed.

"Well, we did it, didn't we?" said Frost, dropping back on his bed, very tired. "He's a great man," he added, "he knows what power is and isn't afraid to take hold of it. He's a great man, all right."

It was about quarter to five. The talk had lasted nearly an hour and a half. Frost had forgotten to give Khrushchev the copy of *In the Clearing* which he had brought for him.

"Robert," I said, "don't you want to sign the book?" "Oh, I forgot, didn't I?" he said. "Yeh, I better, hadn't I?"

I rushed out and asked Surkov to ask the Premier to wait a moment, Frost wanted to give him his book. Back upstairs, Frost was getting set to inscribe the book but he couldn't remember Khrushchev's title. He finally put down:

> *To Premier Khrushchev*
> *from his rival in friendship*
> *Robert Frost*
>
> *Gagra*
> *Sept 7 1962*

I took it downstairs and handed it to Khrushchev, who was sitting beside the driver in a green, open Chaika convertible. His secretary and doctor were in back. The escort was a short way off. For a moment it seemed improbable, there in that lush, azure world, that the dramatic meeting which we all had been at had actually occurred. Power affects everyone who handles it; it rubs off what you touch and stains you. Great power seems fantastic — its source is so general that there seems to be no source at all. And the values behind it, as Frost often said, lie in a man's performance.

There were a number of things Frost went to Russia for. The more any of us thinks back on it, though, the more we see it as a dramatization of the terms by which we honor excellence and, in honoring it, engage it to serve us.

Frost was a famous man, a famous institution, long before he went to Russia. Literary honors encouraged in him a sense of urgency about political control or, bluntly, power. He went to Russia, so he hoped from the start, to see Khrushchev, to talk to the man in charge. He wanted to talk about his notion of the inevitable course of civilization and what he believed the Caesars of our world had to do. The honors he received made him nervous, for honor, of course, may be terrifying: it may mean you have to do something better the next time, something which you fear you will fail — as Frost feared he would fail on his trip to Gagra.

He went to Russia with the notion that the Russians were

a lot of peasants, a landful of bears, but they out-honored him. They honored him sincerely out of respect for his skill, so that when he went to Gagra he went with a special sense of intensity, devotion, obligation, and inevitability. He went with a certain irreverence, that special responsibility of the honored man.

Khrushchev, the most powerful political figure in Russia, acknowledged his responsibility for maintaining cultural tradition. Frost, at his death the most venerated literary man in America, acknowledged his responsibility for shaping the forces of power in the world. The two men talked freely, irreverently, with deep respect and high intensity. They discussed the East-West alignment of power; they told anecdotes; they analyzed the meaning of economic competition; they complimented each other on their vitality; they decried the horrors of war and insisted on the necessity of using force to maintain control, to preserve pride, to assert tradition.

Khrushchev, who said he hated the treacherous Nazis, praised capitalist American technical skill. Frost, who said the Chinese and Africans amounted to nothing in the structure of the world, admired the accomplishments of Russian socialism. Together they agreed that Russia and the United States must cease all pettiness, must be grand.

What remains of this meeting, as of Frost's whole trip to Russia, is the dramatic confrontation of two irreverent and much-honored men, each of whom was more affected by the other man than most people suppose. The power of skill is that it commands respect.

Particularly disappointing to Frost was the tendency of some of the American press to sensationalize his trip. He was unhappy that his reading of "Mending Wall" had been interpreted as commentary on Berlin. He was discomfited that reporters who quoted him straight seemed sometimes to use his words in ways he hadn't meant them. Right after the next day's press conference at which he called Khrushchev a ruffian, he asked me if he had been understood. He said he meant rough-and-ready; he meant the word in its northern Vermont sense of praise for the energetic, audacious, and virile man who comes down from the hills on Saturday night and has the courage and skill to pick the town up by the scruff of its neck.

And then later he was deeply disturbed both by the way his own use of the word "liberal" was analyzed, and by the interpretation of his remark that Khrushchev had told him that Americans were too liberal to fight.

Plunged into a press conference at Idlewild, just off the plane and tired after two weeks on the road and a seventeen-hour trip home, Frost may appear to have put his foot in it, so to speak, in quoting Khrushchev as he did. But he had expressed many times before this press conference both his own attitude toward liberalism and the attitude he understood Khrushchev to be taking. He believed that the world today is dominated not so much by ideals and "isms" as by actual power balance. He urged that his country be ready ultimately to risk its own defense and be willing always to make every gesture of magnanimity. Political power, cultural excellence, and moral integrity were, for him, inseparable. Those "liberals" who lacked his strength of conviction seemed to him, as he put it, sapheads. He didn't admire them. He deeply admired Khrushchev, a card-carrying member of the Communist Party — "he's our enemy and he's a great man" — for the drive and purposefulness of his vision of power.

In the fall of 1962 the controversy around the "too liberal to fight" phrase exceeded reasonable proportions. Few people understood what Frost had said or what his position was. None of the commentators in Washington showed that they understood. Some men argued that the phrase meant the Russians were confident that the Americans wouldn't defend by arms "certain values which are negotiable." Others said the phrase meant that Khrushchev feared "the United States will fight because the liberals are too weak to prevent it."

In a letter addressed to Norman Thomas in reply to a note from him, but never finished, Frost went right to the center of the controversy, as he had a number of times in private conversation and as he suggested in his reading at the Library of Congress in October. He indicated that Khrushchev's and his own understanding of "liberalism" was directly connected with nobility of performance and actual expression of political control. They admired each other as men who dared do and say what they believed correctly human.

Everyone seemed to want to start joking with me about the word "liberal" but as you say it's no joking matter. It was almost that with Khrushchev. Shall I try to tell you the affable way he used it with me in Gagra. He was just being good-natured and literary when he expressed concern for American liberality. He was quoting either Gorky to Tolstoi or Tolstoi to Gorky, I forget which, when he said there was such a thing possibly as a nation's getting like the bald-headed row at a leg show so it enjoyed wanting to do what it could no longer do. I was interested to find the great old powerhouse so bookish. People have asked me if he was literary like Kennedy and you and me. I think I broke down his figure by answering we were too young a nation for that worry.

There are all sorts of liberals and I have amused myself with defining them. Khrushchev's was a good crack. My own latest is that they are people who have had the liberal education that I fled and have come back to assert my difference with in their own strong-holds, the colleges. If Matthew Arnold is their gospel, I come pretty near being liberal myself. I have teasingly described them as people who can't take their own side in a quarrel and would rather fuss with a Gordian knot than cut it and as "Dover Beach-combers" and as Matthew Arnold's wisest "who take dejectedly their seat upon the intellectual throne." They are never arbitrary enough "to bid their will avouch it" like a real leader. But all that aside after it has enter-tained you enough, I yield to no one in my admiration for the kind of liberal you have been, you and Henry Wallace. One of the great moments of my life was when we three foregathered at Larry Spivak's party and I stood between you and Henry for a chance photographer to take our picture. My son-in-law had been rebuking Henry for going to China when Hull had warned him not to go. Henry had already admitted he shouldn't have gone. My son-in-law had dispersed in the crowd and I had put my hand on Henry's shoulder in affectionate sympathy. Then you came along and there we three stood in a row against the world. I treasure the picture and if you want these sentiments signed I'll come and have a talk with you whenever you're inclined. I can't see how Khrushchev's talk got turned into what you quote that we weren't men enough to fight. I came nearer than he to threatening: with my native geniality I assured him that we were no more afraid of him than he was of us. We seemed in perfect agreement that we shouldn't come to blows till we were sure there was a big issue remaining between us, of his kind of democracy versus our kind of democracy, approximating each other as they are, his by easing downward towards socialism from the severity of its original ideals, ours by straining upward towards socialism through various phases of welfare state-ism. I said the stage or arena is set between us for a rivalry of perhaps a hundred years. Let's hope we can take it out in sports, science, art, business, and politics before ever we have to take it out in the bloody politics of war. It was all magnanimity — Aristotle's great word. I should have expected you to approve. Liberal in a good sense of the word. Browning tells of a post office bulletin notice in Italy "two liberal thieves were shot." If only a word would stay put in basic English.

This may seem part of history now, although the principles involved bear down on us today more, not less, acutely. It seems to me still as close and vivid as the meeting at Gagra, as Frost lying on his bed after the meeting, exhausted, his temperature normal again. It seems as close as the drive to the airport — we missed the plane — and the night spent in a tiny, hot room before the morning flight back to Moscow. It seems still as close as Frost, in the hospital, saying that he wanted to go back to Russia to see Khrushchev because they had understood each other. It will always seem as close as the letter I have which tells how we teamed up. "Didn't we ride Hell-bent back from Gagra after toasts to miss our plane?"

SATURDAY

The next plane brought us into Moscow at noon Saturday. We all talked casually on the way up, though Frost mostly dozed. Surkov talked about Russian literature and about some things that would soon be published. Demyan Bedny's poetry, he said, would be revived, and in mid-1963 in the Poet's Library series there would be a volume of Pasternak, a volume larger than the 1961 edition which Surkov had edited. And I understood from him what many of us had heard from others, that Khrushchev personally has played not only a decisive but also a vital role in the revival of Russian literature. Ehrenburg's memoirs were to continue to be published, for, although all biography exaggerates and prettifies, according to the Premier, the memoirs were "engaging and useful," important documents about a period nobody else knew so well from that point of view. During the winter to follow there was a sharp intellectual conflict, but by the end of summer of 1963 Khrushchev's moderating influence seemed to be favoring the liberals again, to take that word in a different sense — those writers who cared to keep up close contacts with Western Europe and to write openly about life at home. Nekrasov had not been expelled by the Party; Ehrenburg still played a central, bellwether role in the conflict; and Tvardovsky's eminence, influence and integrity were recognized by the long-awaited publication of the satiric poem *Vassily Tyorkin in the Next World*, a narrative in verse about Tvardovsky's Great Patriotic War tank hero, Tyorkin, up in Heaven, which turns out to be a copy of the Soviet bureaucracy. I like to think that Frost's talk with Khrushchev and Khrushchev's pledge to stop the name-calling and the propaganda helped improve the conditions of our world.

Frost was greeted at the Moscow airport as if he were the Prodigal Son. Yevtushenko and Simonov had been stand-ins for him at a scheduled poetry reading the evening before. Over a thousand persons had crowded into the auditorium of the Lenin Pedagogical Institute in Moscow and had heard

Yevtushenko and Simonov read poems by Frost and poems to him and talk about his poetry. Nobody had known until after the last minute that we had, indeed, missed our plane and that there would be none until nine the next morning. Back in Moscow the Prodigal Son had barely time to eat a sandwich before the press swarmed in.

The press conference, in Frost's room in the hotel, was attended by some sixty or seventy reporters. There were microphones and television and newsreel cameras. Frost spoke distinctly but not always clearly. He missed a number of questions, and many of his answers consisted more of what, under such pressure, he suddenly felt he ought to say than of what he knew had been said. Besides, a poet's imagination makes real words for us where we otherwise think we find only deserts or prisons. Frost's remark that Khrushchev was a ruffian slipped from that real world into the world of public statements — in the hubbub of voices and cameras, a reporter's query if that was what he actually meant was never heard by Frost, or he ignored it, you couldn't always tell — and people took it their way, literally. They did Frost a disservice. In the same way, I think, those who misunderstood Frost's admiration for Khrushchev and for Russia must now acknowledge that they were then being parochial. As Frost said, in October after his trip, at the National Poetry Festival in the Library of Congress, "The greatest expression in all slang expressions is 'you bet your sweet life.' If you aren't ready to bet your sweet life, however sweet, you're no gambler." Lest there be any doubt how he felt about his new Russian friends, Frost later said, "I'm going to send some presents to the poets over there. Fine fellows. I'm going to send some silver from the Revolutionary War. Our Revolutionary War, and mark them as such." What did he make of all the politics? "We're playing a great world game with some style, I tell you," he said. At this press conference in his hotel room, when asked about cultural exchanges, he said, "It's good when you have them going both ways. But the big thing," he added, "is magnanimity, our countries' being rivals in magnanimity." That's what his trip was all about.

That Saturday afternoon he gave a poetry reading at the American Embassy for members of the staff and their children. "Hello, you damn Yankees," he said and went on from there. The small audience were special fans. Even those who rarely read a poem felt briefly close to the best of America.

There was tea at the McSweeneys', and then Mrs. McSweeney and Frost went on their shopping spree in downtown Moscow.

The trip was almost over. Several times during it, when rather depressed, discouraged about the chances of seeing Khrushchev or about his own success, Frost had thought and talked about the people back in Boston closest to him and what a fool they must think him to have agreed to a junket like this. Now, after conspicuous success, he thought of them with bright-eyed warmth, for he did, indeed, have something to show. He, too, was sensible of the triumph of his trip. This made him all the more impatient to be quickly back in his familiar world, at ease and at work again.

But our plane left only the next morning. This final evening we were to dine at the Tvardovskys', a sort of symbolic farewell meant to promise reunion soon. Even though that reunion never occurred, the evening may stand as the warm Russian testimonial to Frost's accomplishments on his tour. The Tvardovskys, in the company of Surkov and his wife, Demichev (from the editorial board of *New World*) and his wife, the film director Kozintsev, whom we had met in Leningrad, and the editor of the magazine *Iskusstvo* (Art), set a lavish Russian table and in family style pressed on Frost the warmest Russian hospitality. Mrs. Tvardovsky even gave Frost some marinated mushrooms to take home with him.

In the middle of the evening, while everyone was seated around the oblong table in the dining room, there in the Tvardovsky's apartment by the Moscow River, the television was turned on. We watched *Boris Godunov* for a while as we ate hors d'oeuvres and drank soup. And then suddenly, there on the screen, was Frost. A twenty-minute excerpt from his hour-long show had been specially prepared for transmission after the first act this evening, so that Frost himself could see it. It was a very fine recording; Frost, Surkov and Yevtushenko made an excellent impression; everyone was highly pleased. The full recording was subsequently shown several times over the Moscow station and was, I hear, a great success. Frost had read his poems to hundreds, reached thousands through reports in the papers, and been seen my millions on TV. Artistically meritorious, his trip was a popular success. He did in Russia what he had long before done in his own country. As he said to a Russian reporter the next morning at the airport, when asked for a final comment on his stay: "The Writers Union has made this trip one of the most significant events in my life. I've had a chance to express admiration for your mighty country, whose fate it is to be our rival in the years ahead. I gratefully acknowledge your generous hospitality." He paused. "I've spoken about these feelings many times — in Moscow, in Leningrad, and in Gagra." With a wave of his hand and a smile, he said good-by to Matlock, to Surkov and Tvardovsky, to Zenkevich and Kashkin, to the guides, to the reporters, and, beside Stewart Udall who had stayed over a day in order to go home with him, walked up the ramp into the Soviet jet that would take us to Paris.

The next day *Pravda* ran Frost's picture, four new translations of his poems, and a long article by Surkov summing up Frost's visit, ending:

I . . . was left with the impression that we were seeing off an honest and true friend, one who in may ways understands a solution to the most important issues of our time quite differently from us but who sincerely wishes to purge reciprocal relations between peoples of the USA and the USSR of everything superficial and biased, to work for friendship, mutual understanding and trust.

We wish that Robert Frost may defend his ideals of peaceful competition of the two systems with just such youthful energy as that with which his verse resounds, as that which he displayed on meeting Soviet people.

By teatime Sunday we were back in New York, "Us and Russia," Frost said on the flight back as he said many other times, "that might take a couple hundred years before it's finished. That's one of the hard things about dying, wondering how all the unfinished business will come out." When a reporter at the press conference at Idlewild asked if he planned to visit Russia again, Frost quipped, "Yes, when I'm older and wiser."

AND AFTER

THE WHITE HOUSE

WASHINGTON

September 13, 1962

DEAR MR. FROST:

I am among the many millions of your countrymen who have been proud and delighted by your remarks and observations on your trip through the Soviet Union. You did wonderfully. You helped set a framework for broad and magnanimous discussion.

I am sure that on both sides of the Iron Curtain your visit will be long remembered.

Cordially yours,

AUGUST HECKSCHER

Special Consultant on the Arts

I saw Frost on New Year's Day, 1963. Our children had sent him a note and drawn a calendar with a picture for the board at the foot of his hospital bed. He and I drank champagne and toasted the New Year in. He talked about politics and the necessity for "unscrupulous high-mindedness." He damned the State Department an extra time and said that all politicians were just playing little games. He felt weak and uncertain, but he said he wanted to see Katayev again, as soon as he arrived, for me to be sure to let Katayev know. Katayev did see him in the hospital a few weeks later and said he was happy to have shaken Frost's hand. "If all humanity had men like Frost," he was quoted as saying, "there would be no more wars." And Frost was quoted as having said to Katayev about Khrushchev: "We were charmed with each other. I'm very fond of him. He's a lovable man. I could talk out to him and he could talk out to me. It's a grand time to be alive," he added, "to see two rivalries drawing up for the next hundred years in the world and to see them do it in a somewhat civilized way. Khrushchev and I, we met on the basis of honor and decency in the old-fashioned way, in the way of sports and all the way up. It was a very splendid thing and nothing like it ever happened to me." "My main idea with Khrushchev and elsewhere," Frost had written me three months before, "[was] that as Russia had eased down from the severity of its doctrine towards Socialism and we had strained upward through phases of Welfare Statism towards Socialism the two nations may have approximated to where they can shake hands now and then — socially."

And as we saw the first day of the New Year go by in the hospital in Boston, Frost kept talking about wanting to go back to Russia, about getting well again and going over to see Khrushchev for one more conversation, one more talk to straighten things out. He'd been writing poetry but he said it was no good. He was close to giving up, he said, meaning dying. "You have the world before you," he said. "It's a good world, Robert," I said. And he agreed that life is worth living, that he had a lot to do, that he wanted to come down and see us and write up something on his Russian trip. "You give your own version of our trip to Moscow," he said. And I said I didn't think it would be much different from his, if you took everything into account. At least, I wouldn't mean it to be. The angle would be different; I couldn't help that.

In a letter which he dictated in the fall after his return but never finished and which is now in the Baker Library at Dartmouth, Frost summed up the meaning of his experiences:

. . . I found the Russians a great people, good-natured in their confidence that peaceful coexistence (their word, not mine) might be a better way than war (their word, not mine) to win the ultimate victory for the workers of the world. I found them as determined to beat us as I think we are to beat them in sports, in art, in science, in business, in democracy, in chivalry and magnanimity (large not petty mindedness). There was nothing common or mean in my conversation with the Prime Minister or with Surkov, the Secretary of the Union of Soviet Writers, who wrote the *Pravda* article a first-rate man, one of the best people I talked with. But neither of us blinked the realities. We are paired off for prevailure. The Prime Minister teased me a little about our shrinking dollar and our loss of the oceans as protection. With a slight irony he said we ought to be pleased with their surpassing us in hydro-electric power because they had learned the engineering from us. Some time I could tell you more of my vain proposal to him about Berlin. . . . If great wars start in little squabbles, measures must be taken about the squabbles. . . . I could see they were not afraid of us. Ours is a God-ordained rivalry. I went so far as to acknowledge Khrushchev's power to his face, and I said I would be willing to welcome any simple solution of Berlin as coming from him. . . .

A close friend of Frost's of very long standing has pointed out how a phrase in the letter echoes two lines from Marvell which Frost often quoted with utmost admiration:

> He nothing common did or mean
> Upon that memorable scene.

On our trip, that "he" was Frost.

By coincidence, as strange as the coincidences in Dostoevsky novels and, afterwards, seemingly as inevitable, Adams and I dined with Katayev and Rozov, among others, in New York on January 28. After dinner, Adams and I talked at his apartment until past midnight about our trip to Russia and about our friend, Adams's old friend, my new one. The six o'clock hospital bulletin, broadcast over the radio, had given depressing news. We sat talking with the ghostly feeling that very possibly — but how could you know? — Robert Frost was dead. About an hour later, he was.

I don't wish to seem either sentimental or pretentious but, you know, I'd had a feeling a number of times on the trip that Frost was prefiguring his own death. He had long worried about his health. He had been sick. And he kept reading his latest poems, including "Away." It seemed then, as one would like to think it actual now, that this was a fillip to his life, the last greatest play of wit that would bring him and our dead friends to life again. For with whimsy and love, he said:

> *And I may return*
> *If dissatisfied*
> *With what I learn*
> *From having died.*

The last poem in Frost's last book ends:

> *I see for Nature no defeat*
> *In one tree's overthrow*
> *Or for myself in my retreat*
> *For yet another blow.*

The poem was written some time before the trip, but Frost said it often there, and it still stands, to cite Frost's words, "after the time of our lives in Russia," as a promise we must now promise ourselves.

Notes

F.D. Reeve

Over My Shoulder

4   Quoted in Louis Untermeyer, *Robert Frost: a Backward Look,* Washington, D. C.: The Library of Congress, 1964, p. 23

5   *Ibid*

7   from Wade Van Dore's memoir *Robert Frost and Wade Van Dore: the Life of the Hired Man* as given by Dan Toomey, "Gestures against the Grain," Marlboro College, 28 September 2000.

10 "The Constant Symbol," preface to *The Poems of Robert Frost,* New York: The Modern Library, 1946, p. xvii

13 *Ibid*, p. xix

Monday

21 Anatoly Dobrynin: Anatoly Fyodorovich Dobrynin (b.1919) was appointed ambassador to the United States in 1962, elected a member of the Central Committee of the Communist Party in 1971, and a secretary in 1986. Long an advocate of détente, and one of the most influential voices in U.S.-U.S.S.R. relations, he published a summary of his quarter century in Washington: *In Confidence: Moscow's Ambassador to America's Six Cold War Presidents (1962-1986)*, Lawrence Malkin, ed, New York: Crown, 1995.

21 Stewart Udall: Stewart Lee Udall (b.1920) was appointed Secretary of the Interior by Presidents Kennedy and Johnson. He now practices as an environmental lawyer in New Mexico. In his book *The Myths of August* (New Brunswick:Rutgers Univer-

sity Press, 1994) he details (pp 11-14) his own perspective on traveling to Russia with Frost.

21 Frederick B. Adams: Frederick B. Adams (b.1908) was director of the Morgan Library from 1948 through 1969. He delivered an account of the trip from a bibliophile's point of view, which was published as *To Russia with Frost*, Boston: The Club of Odd Volumes, 1963. Adams now lives in France.

21 After Frost rejected the State Department's suggestion that it send one of its women translators with him, Frost's secretary Kathleen Morrison turned to the poet William Meredith, who recommended me. At first I was reluctant, for it looked like a sightseeing tour with perhaps a couple of poetry readings tossed in. Couldn't it be more? If I arranged meetings with some of the writers I had met the previous year, couldn't it be a genuine cultural exchange? Mrs. Morrison and Frost agreed.

I might add that because of the intensity of the trip "Mr. Frost" soon turned into "Robert," and, soon after the trip, the Morrisons became "Ted" and "K." In Russia I addressed everyone by first name and patronymic except the young poets, all of whom used only a first name or a nickname.

TUESDAY

27 MacDowell Medal: A lifetime achievement award named for the composer Edward MacDowell and given annually by the MacDowell Colony in Peterborough, New Hampshire, to a prominent figure who has made an outstanding contribution to the arts.

WEDNESDAY

31   Thomas: Edward Thomas: Edward Thomas (1878-1917) an
English poet, four years younger than Frost and friend of Walter
de la Mare and Joseph Conrad, had dropped out of Oxford to
marry his pregnant childhood sweetheart and had since made
his living as a literary hack. He was often neurasthenically de-
spondent — and, like Frost, suicidal. From October 1913 until
Thomas left for the war, the two shared profound, mutual admiration. Thomas warmly and anonymously reviewed *A Boy's
Will*, and Frost persuaded Thomas to rededicate himself to verse,
pointing out that Thomas's *Pursuit of Spring* was really poetry,
not prose. Thomas was killed at Vimy Ridge.

31   Abercrombie: Lascelles Abercrombie (1881-1938) was a
Gloucestershire poet whom Frost had met in London in the fall
of 1913, (about the time he lunched with Robert Bridges, the
Poet Laureate) and to whom he was so attracted that he moved
his family to Gloucestershire to be near him, the center of a
group of Georgian poets. Abercrombie responded with friendship and a very favorable review of *North of Boston*, and, when
the Frosts revisited England in 1928, an invitation to read at
Leeds, where Abercrombie, aged and diabetic, was then lecturing. On his trip to England in 1957, Frost returned for a day to
his Gloucestershire haunts, but of the old group he was the only
one still living.

32   O'Connor's Weekly: By *O'Connor's Weekly*, Frost was referring
to *T. P.'s Weekly*, whose "Highways and Byways" columnist

steered Frost first to a bungalow in Beaconsfield, where the family settled in early autumn 1912, and then to David Nutt and Company, publishers of such poets as W.E. Henley, where David's brother Alfred's French-born widow had become director.

34 The Inauguration of the President in 1961: For the inauguration of John F. Kennedy, Udall proposed that Kennedy ask Frost to say something and they agreed to ask him to read a poem. At the last minute, Frost composed a piece called "Dedication" as preamble to an older poem, "The Gift Outright." Udall had introduced Frost to Kennedy in 1959. the poet and the president remained on terms of mutual admiration up to the end of the Russian trip.

35 Alexander Tvardovsky: Alexander Trifonovich Tvardovsky (1910-1971) was the liberal editor of the literary magazine *Novy mir* from 1950 to 1954 and again from 1958 to 1970. Both times, political repression forced his resignation. More than any one else, he rehabilitated Russian literature in the post-Stalin era. A loyal Party member but a stalwart believer in truth, the winner of many literary prizes, he was famous for the long poems *The Land of Muravia* and *Vassily Tyorkin*. His magazine published such honored but anathematized writers as Pasternak, Babel, Akhmatova and Mandelshtam, and introduced Solzhenitsyn, Voinovich, Sinyavsky, Grekova, and Viktor Nekrasov. In 1963, despite his own vacillating health, he published the rollicking, satiric epic *Tyorkin in the Next World*, in which Heaven turns out to be run by the same bumbling bunch of crooked

cronies as the U. S. S. R. Translations of his work are available in the Moscow-published *Selected Poetry*, 1981.

35 Alexei Surkov: Alexei Aleksandrovich Surkov (1899-1983) was both a poet and a Party functionary in the literary field from 1928 until his death. For the last thirty years of his life, he served as First Secretary of the Soviet Writers' Union and a member of the Supreme Soviet. He wrote many lyrics on patriotic themes and published extensively. From 1944 to 1946, he edited the Writers' Union official newspaper *Literaturnaya gazeta*, and, from 1945 to 1953, the magazine *Ogonyok*. In 1958, after *Doctor Zhivago* was published abroad, he led the expulsion of Pasternak from the Writers' Union; his editing a volume of Pasternak's poems was the work of a make-peace.

35 Writers Union: The Union of Writers of the U.S.S.R. was the only nation-wide, official organization of writers and critics. Established on April 23, 1932, by the Communist Party Central Committee, it replaced all previous literary groupings and controlled the Gorky Literary Institute and all major literary periodicals. Membership, open to candidates who had published two books and were supported by three members, was compulsory for a literary career; expulsion meant being blacklisted, as Akhmatova, Pasternak and Solzhenitsyn knew only too well. Like all other official organizations, the Union provided many fringe benefits for its members, ranging from access to special housing in Peredelkino outside Moscow and Komarovo outside Leningrad, to special medical care, rest homes and Black Sea

resorts, and trips abroad. Mikhail Bulgakov brilliantly satirized its bureaucratic pomposity and self-serving pretentiousness in his novel *The Master and Margarita*.

35 Yevgeny Yevtushenko: Yevgeny Aleksandrovich Yevtushenko (b.1933) was a literary success before he turned twenty. His first book of poems appeared while he was still a student at the Gorky Literary Institute, and a volume followed almost every year thereafter. A long poem, "Zima Junction," appeared in 1956. The most notorious of the "young Turks" fighting entrenched literary and political values, he provoked great controversy with his poems "Babyi Yar" in 1961 and "Stalin's Heirs" in 1962. From 1962 to 1969 he served on the editorial board of the magazine *Yunost*, and in 1967 became a member of the Presidium of the Writers' Union. When the Soviet Union dissolved, literary censorship disappeared. Poets and writers were no longer expected to express openly dissident views. The marketplace rapidly took over determining the quantity and quality of books published. Many writers, artists (and scientists!) joined exiled colleagues in the West. Some, like Yevtushenko, continue to publish and to maintain a residence in Russia while earning their living by teaching in the States.

His work is available in translation in *The Collected Poems 1952-1990*, edited by Albert C. Todd with the author and James Ragan, New York: Henry Holt/a John Macrae Book, 1991.

35 Mikhail Zenkevich: Mikhail Aleksandrovich Zenkevich (1891-1973) was a member of the Acmeist generation. In the Twen-

ties, his poetry gave way to translation to earn a living. The last book of his own work appeared in 1962. Some of his new translations of Frost appeared in *Izvestiya* and *Pravda* during Frost's visit; his anthology of translations of Frost, *Iz devyati knig* (From Nine Books), the following year.

35 Ivan Kashkin: Ivan Aleksandrovich Kashkin (1899-1963) was a Moscow professor whose sensitive readings of English and American poetry educated a whole generation in the nuances of well-crafted verse. His Frost translations appeared in *Literatura i zhizn* and in anthologies.

35 ... two women: Freda Lurye and Yelena Romanova were assigned to Frost as guides and translators. Fred Adams nicknamed them "the pendragons" because of their constant interference, their effort to make Frost a tourist, and their obvious role as informers. The following January, Lurye "guided" the playwright Victor Rozov and the novelist Valentin Katayev on a trip to New York and Boston, where they called on Frost in the hospital. When I ran across Lurye in Moscow thirty years later, she, who valued her literary connections, indirectly apologized for the kind of service she had performed.

35 *One Day in the Life of Ivan Denisovich,* a novella, Solzhenitsyn's first literary work, was published in the November 1962 issue of *Novy mir,* two months after Frost's visit. It was the first work to expose in public literature conditions in the forced-labor camps of the "Gulag."

36 Pasternak: Boris Leonidovich Pasternak (1890-1960) known the

world over for his novel *Doctor Zhivago*, became an established major poet with his third collection *Sestra moya zhizn* (My Sister Life), 1922. *Spektorsky*, a novel in verse published in 1931, expressed his ambivalence about the Revolution of 1917. During the last thirty years of his life he translated extensively; his versions of Shakespeare are now standard in the Russian theater. *Doctor Zhivago* came out in the West in 1957, the same year as his final book of poems, *Kogda razgulyaetsya* (When the Storm Clears). In 1958, he first accepted and then under great pressure declined the Nobel Prize. Thousands attended his funeral in Peredelkino, where his grave is still a site of pilgrimage.

36 "Babyi Yar": Evtushenko's poem published in September 1961 confronted Soviet anti-Semitism by embracing as a central image the ravine near Kiev where German soldiers had massacred Jews.

39 Sovietskaya Hotel: The hotel has taken back its old name, "Yar," although it has not recaptured past grandeur. The "yar" in Yevtushenko's poem is a "pit" or "ravine." The "yar" (yar + a soft sign) that was the restaurant and is the hotel means verdigris, the lovely color of oxidized copper.

39 Terry Catherman: Terrence F. Catherman (1925-1999) began with the State Department in 1950 in Germany, served in Washington, Vienna — and then as cultural officer in Moscow. Afterwards, he went on to a newly reunited Germany as Deputy Public Affairs Officer.

39 Jack Matlock: Jack Foust Matlock (b.1929), George F. Kennan

Professor at the Institute for Advanced Study, taught Russian at Dartmouth in the early 1950s. Working with the Foreign Service, he left Russia for Africa in 1963, but later returned to Europe and served as ambassador to Czechoslovakia in the early 1980s, as Senior Director for Europe and the USSR on the staff of the National Security Council (1983-86) and then as ambassador to the U.S.S.R. from 1987 through 1991. After leaving the Foreign Service in 1991, he was a senior research fellow (91-93) and then a faculty member (Davis Professor) at Columbia University (93-96). He wrote his own account of the collapse of the Soviet Union, *Autopsy on an Empire* (New York: Random House, 1995) which gives the most responsive, reliable eyewitness account of the devolution of the U. S. S. R.

40 ...what happened to artists and writers during the winter after Frost's visit: During the winter after Frost's visit, Khrushchev's power faltered. Cultural repression set in again. The liberalizing trend that followed Stalin's death in 1953 and culminated in the 22nd Party Congress's condemnation of Stalin in 1961 — "The Thaw" — was stopped cold. Beginning with a Party Central Committee meeting in November, conservatives spoke out against "formalist tendencies" in the arts. On December 1, Khrushchev visited an art exhibit at Moscow's Manezh where he called one of the modern paintings "shit." On the 17th, intellectuals held a stormy protest meeting, but repressive measures escalated. The winter of 1963 saw one backward step after another. During the remainder of the 1960s, a number of writers (Sinyavsky, Daniel) began publishing abroad, or underground (*samizdat*). Conditions of censorship, foreign exile and sentencing to hard labor prevailed throughout the "Period of Stagnation," that is, until the end of the Soviet era.

40 Chukovsky: Korney Ivanovich Chukovsky (1882-1969) whose real name was Nikolai Vasilievich Korneichukov, was reared by his peasant mother in Ukraine and never finished school. He began work as a reporter for an Odessa newspaper, which sent him to England in 1903-1904, where he began what became fluency in English. He was the first to translate Whitman into Russian (1907). First allied with the Symbolists and then with the writers and painters in the village of Kuokkala outside St. Petersburg, he became a scholar of the nineteenth-century poet Nikolai Nekrasov, a fervid and scrupulous translator, a devotee of limpid Russian opposed to contemporary bureaucratese, and a children's writer whose verse tales such as "The Crocodile," "The Telephone," and "Doctor Ouch!" remain unsurpassed. He was awarded a Russian doctoral degree in 1957 and a D.Litt. by Oxford the spring before Frost met him. After Gorky's death in 1936, he took over helping many writers in jeopardy; he spoke out in support of dissidents like young Brodsky, and at personal risk sheltered Solzhenitsyn.

His children's poems are too idiomatic to translate, but his book about children's speech, *From Two to Five*, is available and also his *The Art of Translation*.

40 Paustovsky: Konstantin Georgievich Paustovsky (1892-1968) a

169

Cossack by descent, studied at Kiev and Moscow Universities, began writing stories before World War I, and published his first collection in 1925. During the 1920s, he kicked around Russia working all sorts of odd jobs. During the Great Patriotic War (World War II) while others were publishing uplifting propaganda, he wrote a novel about the intelligentsia on the eve of the war, *Dym otechestva* (Smoke of the Fatherland). In the two decades following the war, he wrote a number of works, none more important than his reminiscences, *Povest o zhizni* (Story of a Life, translated in 1964-69 and again in 1982). At the same time, he served as editor of two anthologies of fresh, new work, *Literary Moscow* (1956) and *Tarusa Pages* (1961). His public support of both Sinyavsky and Daniel in 1966 earned him the undying admiration of contemporary writers.

THURSDAY

43 ...the huge swimming pool: This swimming pool was constructed on the site of the Cathedral of Christ the Savior, built (1837-1883) to commemorate the victory over Napoleon. The Russian government painstakingly reconstructed the cathedral in 1999 as a symbol of resurgent Russian — as opposed to Soviet — history.

44 Mikoyan: Anastas Ivanovich Mikoyan (1895-1978) was First Deputy Premier at the time of Frost's visit. Subsequently he became Chairman of the Presidium of the Supreme Soviet.

44 On our drive . . . back to our hotel: Many streets have been

renamed: Kropotkin Street is again Prechistenka; Herzen Street has rebecome Bolshaya Nikitskaya; and Gorky Street is again Tverskaya.

45 Tass: The official news agency of the Soviet Union, now RITA-TASS.

51 S. M. Alyansky: Samuil Mironovich Alyansky was a publisher and art historian. In the 1920s in Petrograd his firm was a leading art-and-poetry house. He himself was a close friend of many writers, including Alexander Blok. (See Alyansky's critical study *On the Figure of Christ in "The Twelve"*).

FRIDAY

55 Andrei Sergeyev: Andrei Yakovlevich Sergeyev (1933-1998) was respected as an excellent translator of Frost. During Frost's visit, he published translations of Frost in *Literaturnaya gazeta* and other journals. A volume of them — *Izbrannya Lirika* (Selected Poems) — came out in 1968. He also published his own postmodern short fictions, but as far as I know, a proposed book of them remained uncompleted.

66 Stepan Shchipachev: Stepan Petrovich Shchipachev (1898-1979) served twenty-two years in the Red Army before discovering his facility with rhyme, easy imagery and popular themes ("Song of Moscow," 1968). When censorship eased in 1961-62, Shchipachev, a Writers' Union functionary, leaned toward the Left, too, but in 1963 he was dropped from his post for "revisionism." He published a book of translations of Frost, *Tol'ko izbrannoe*, the year Frost came.

66 Julian Oksman: Yulian Grigorievich Oksman (1894-1970)
the most outspoken Russian humanist, specialized in the literature and culture of the first half of the nineteenth century. A
professor at Petrograd University from 1923 to1933, he was
then executive director of the Institute of Russian Literature until
1936, when he was definitively arrested under the infamous Article 58 (he had previously been detained and questioned desul-
torily from 1929 on) and sentenced to hard labor in Magadan
for ten years, to be followed by perpetual exile. After the labor
camp, he taught at Saratov University until he was rehabilitated and returned to the capital. Prominent among his books
are *From "The Captain's Daughter" to "A Sportsman's Notebook"*
and *Chronicle of Belinsky's Life and Work*. On his return to Moscow, he was appointed a senior researcher at the Institute of
World Literature, where his dynamism and philological leader-
ship established high standards for editions and studies of the
Russian classics. A fictionalized acount of his life may be found
in my novel *Just Over the Border* (New York: Morrow, 1969).

SATURDAY

69 The school was Moscow District Primary School No. 7 at 39
Taganskaya St. Now it is a small evening middle school, but after
the unsuccessful visit, everyone wanted to forget it.

70 cosmonauts' flight: The Soviet Union launched its first space
vehicle, or *sputnik*, in 1957. Space probes by both Russia
and the United States followed, but the first manned orbital

flight was made by Yuri Gagarin on April 12, 1961. Alan Shepard made a suborbital flight the next month, and John Glenn an orbital flight on February 20, 1962. In August, scarcely two weeks before Frost's visit, Andrian Nikolayev and Pavel Popovich made simultaneous orbital flights in two *Vostok* capsules. The idea of flight had long interested Frost who, in his poem "Kitty Hawk," saw it as an expression of Western, especially American cultural vigor: "We are not the kind/To stay too confined."

72   Café Aelita: This was a so-called "youth café" (named after A.N. Tolstoy's utopian novel *Aelita*) — that is, a clean, well-lighted place where well-to-do people on the way up could meet, chat, dance a little, drink a little wine, and catch up on the latest culture. I don't recall who was there, but I remember the place seemed dead. Compared to a Soho pub in London or to a genuine Parisian café, it was. But since our group almost doubled the number of customers (I'm probably exaggerating) and Yevtushenko loved using the microphone and warming up the audience, we all — even the other Russians — relaxed and had a good time.

72   Komsomol: The Communist Youth League is a membership organization for teens and twenties programmed to prepare them for Party membership.

73   Eduard Mezhelaitis: Eduardas Mieželaitis (1919-1997) was one of the national minority poets who, writing in both Russian and Lithuanian, was part of the dominant literary coterie. From

1959 to 1970 he was Chairman of the Lithuanian Writers' Union. Soon after Frost arrived, *Izvestia* published his poem and tribute to Frost, "The Blue-eyed Cliff," in which he touted Frost for all the standard reasons. A week later, *Pravda* published an article praising Mezhelaitis' image, poem and tribute. I found it interesting and unjust that Mezhelaitis, a well-meaning man in his early forties, was brought along as one of the young poets, but the Russians conspicuously condescended to him. They made clear he wasn't one of them. As far as I know, his work has not been translated into English.

73 Yevgeny Vinokurov: Yevgeny Mikhailovich Vinokurov (b.1925) graduated from the Gorky Literary Institute in 1951, published his first book of poems that year, and a dozen years later joined the Institute's faculty. Of the half dozen young poets bombarding Moscow at the time of Frost's visit, he was the most laconic, the most original, and the most talented. Pasternak much admired his 1956 volume *Sineva* (Sky Blue). A new volume appeared almost every year. *Slovo* (Word) in 1962 was particularly distinguished. His collected essays came out in 1979. His later poetry of the 1970s, 80s and 90s is broader, more skilfully detailed, more complex, and more powerful. Translations of his verse can be found in a number of anthologies — for example, in George Reavey's *The New Russian Poets* 1953-68 (London: Calder & Boyars, 1968).

73 Andrei Voznesensky: Andrei Andreyevich Voznesensky (b.1933) started as an architect with a diploma from the Institute in 1957,

but with the appearance of "The Masters" and "Goya" in 1959 he was launched on a poetic career. *Parabola* and *Mosaic* in 1960 affirmed his position as one of the two leading "young poets." He traveled widely to give poetry readings, his declamatory style being particularly popular in the West. More and more his work was translated, especially the 1964 book *Antiworlds*. Although Khruschev denounced him as a "bourgeois formalist" in 1963, he continued to publish and to perform. In 1967 he was elected to the Presidium of the Writers' Union. His popularity remained undiminished through the 1980s. Dissolution of the U. S. S. R. and the changed economy affected his position. In the spring of 2000, he, who had once defied Khrushchev and the Party and championed younger writers, signed a letter supporting Boris Berezovsky as a cultural patron.

A full and fair selection of his poetry in translation by many hands is *An Arrow in the Wall* , edited by William Jay Smith and F. D. Reeve (New York: Holt, 1987).

78 Robert Rozhdestvensky: Robert Ivanovich Rozhdestvensky (1932-1994) graduated from the Gorky Literary Institute in 1956, the same year his second book of poems came out. *Uninhabited Islands* (1962) and other volumes endeared him to countless audiences as one of the rebellious young poets. He was awarded the Komsomol Prize for Literature in 1972. Translations of his work are most readily found in anthologies.

SUNDAY

83 Konstantin Simonov: Konstantin Mikhailovich Simonov (1915-
1979) was one of the smoothest and ablest operators in the cultural field. He finished the Gorky Literary Institute at the age
of twenty-three and served as a correspondent during The Great
Patriotic War, publishing the first of his Stalingrad trilogy, *Days
and Nights*, in 1943-4. *The Living and the Dead* came out between 1959 and 1971, and the third part, *Soldiers Are Not Born*,
in 1963-4. He also wrote sentimental and propagandistic plays,
of which *The Russians* (1942) is perhaps best known. His wartime lyrics, such as "Wait For Me and I'll Be Back," were hugely
popular and sung everywhere. His success, his Party membership, and his conservative views made him politically appealing
to the established authorities, winning him six Stalin Prizes, a
bunch of others, and election as Writers' Union secretary. During the period of post-War repression, he served as editor of
Novy mir (1946-50 and 1954-58) and of *Literaturnaya
gazeta* (1950-3). I was told he had earned so much money that
the government had granted him an open bank account.

   Much of his work is available in translation, especially the
Stalingrad trilogy.

MONDAY

98 Shvarts's play *The Dragon* had its *première*: Yevgeny Lvovich
Shvarts (1896-1958) was a writer of children's literature and of
powerful, contemporary social satire expressed by retelling in

modern mode famous tales by Andersen and Perrault. *The Naked King* was introduced in 1960. *The Shadow*, briefly staged in 1940, had been produced the year before Frost's visit. Now *The Dragon*, performed as a propaganda vehicle in 1944, was being offered as originally written.

Translations of the plays are available in various anthologies, including *Three Plays*, Avril Pyman, ed., London: Pergamon, 1972.

98 Daniil Granin: Daniil Aleksandrovich Granin (b.1918) was, for the first thirty years of his life, an engineer, and his stories and novels told a lot about technological society, but Granin was also a keen social critic and a quiet, passionate lover of truth, as shown in his 1962 novel *Idu na grozu* (I Face the Storm) and his 1968 story "The House on the Fontanka" with its evocation of Old Russia. Granin was a staunch supporter of younger, dissident writers and of the non-socialist-realist anthologies.

Translations may be found in libraries and in the anthology *Modern Russian Short Stories*, M. Orga, ed., London, 1980.

The unnumbered small dilemmas associated with writing this book are well illustrated by my meeting with Granin twenty-eight years after he had entertained Frost for dinner. Originally, I agreed with Robert not to write about the trip. If he felt like it, he would write something. Even before he died he changed his mind, and after his death the Morrisons asked me to write it up. I cared about being fair to both Russians and Robert — not always easy because of profound cultural differences and different expectations. In an effort to continue to show the American reader how Robert was responding to Russia, I described the evening at the Granins' the way he saw it. Sadly, I deeply offended Daniil Granin.

When we met again some ten years ago, I tried to explain, even to make amends, but Granin's hurt remained inconsolable. I doubt that he understood that Frost, temperamental all his life, was getting antsy about seeing Khrushchev and fed up with tourism, and I think he forgot to what extent the presence of the two women "guides" seriously dampened the responses of any but the boldest or most successful writers. For Granin's sake, I wish I had reported the evening differently.

98 Nikolai Braun: Nikolai Leopoldovich Braun (1902-1975), an established Leningrad poet, published a gathering of six books of lyrics and a long poem "Youth" in a 1962 book titled simply *Poems*. His wife, M. I. Komissarova, was a poet also, and so to this day is their son Nikolai Nikolayevich ("Tricolored Song," 1986) who, for dissident activity, was sentenced to hard labor during the "Period of Stagnation." I met him in St. Petersburg in 1999. His poem "With the Sword of My Speech" is the title poem of a 1997 anthology of St. Petersburg twentieth-century protest poetry.

98 Alexander Popov: Aleksandr Yakovlevich Popov (1913-1968) (penname "Yashin") was one of the first in this period of liberalization to revive the peasant writers and poets' movement that from 1907 to 1937 had celebrated rural Russia. Sergei Yesenin

was lionized in the capitals, but others such as Nikolai Klyuyev, Sergei Klychkov, and Pyotr Oleshin perished in the purges as putative kulak (rich peasant) sympathizers. Popov's rugged prose and verse was fresh and stimulating, like that of Fyodor Abramov or Vasily Belov. Translations of it are now hard to find.

98 Vera Panova: Vera Fyodorovna Panova (1905-1973) a successful journalist and playwright in the 1930s, moved to Leningrad just before the Great Patriotic War. Her first novel, *Sputniki* (Travelers Together, 1945) dramatized individual courage and grit among people on a hospital train. Her second novel, *Rabochy posyolok* (The Factory Village, 1947) looked into the hearts and minds of individual workers. Nevertheless, it, too, won a Stalin Prize. Severe criticism persuaded her to write a work of socialist realism, but then, again, in 1953, she wrote the first post-Stalin novel focusing on individuals — *The Seasons*, this time dealing with bureaucratic corruption. She gave a heart and a face to the required literary norms. In the 1950s she wrote a number of children's books; in the 1960s, historical fiction based on medieval religious themes.

Her first novel, translated as *The Train*, may still be available; the others were translated in the 1970s. Her play *It's Been Ages* can be found in *Contemporary Russian Plays*.

98 Sergei Orlov: Serge Sergeyevich Orlov (1921-1977) was a a reliable but promising poet respected for professional competence and trusted by the Writers' Union.

98 the movie director Kozintsev: Grigory Mikhailovich Kozintsev

(1905-73) for 45 years was one of Russia's extraordinary film-makers, admired for his experiments in the 1920s and for his treatments of the classics from *The Overcoat* (1926) to *Don Quixote* (1957) and *King Lear* (1969). His work was shown in the New York Russian film retrospective in November 2000.

100 Ilya Ehrenburg: Ilya Grigorievich Ehrenburg (1891-1967) was born in Kiev but educated in Moscow where, as a student, he was arrested for revolutionary activities. Released from prison in 1908, he went to Paris, returned to Russia in 1917, again went to the West in 1921, which he roamed as a correspondent for Russian papers until 1941, when he returned to Moscow from German-occupied Paris. His 1922 anti-art satiric novel *The Extraordinary Adventures of Julio Jurenito*, in which the teacher-protagonist calls art the hotbed of anarchism, flouted the principles of proletarian art. Especially after the Great Patriotic War, Ehrenburg was the venerated bellwether of Russian literature. His 1947 novel *The Storm* presented some of the first descriptions of Nazi atrocities, and his 1954 novella *The Thaw* gave its name to the entire post-Stalin artistic renaissance. Portraits in his memoirs *People, Years, Life* (1961-5) of painters, poets, performers and politicians he had known brought back to public memory people who had been purged. Unfortunately, he was too sick to receive Frost, Kornei Chukovksy affirmed over the phone a couple of days later; Frost, who himself had had severe bouts of illness, readily understood.

100 Akhmatova: Anna Andreyevna Akhmatova (penname of Anna

Andreyevna Gorenko) (1889-1966) was, at the time she and Frost met, Russia's outstanding writer. She had come to her position the hard way. She met the poet Nikolai Gumilev in 1903, first published a poem in 1907 in his magazine *Sirius*, hung out with other Acmeists and artists in the fashionable café *Brodyachaya sobaka* (The Stray Dog), married Gumilev in 1910 and lived an arty life in Paris where Modigliani drew a number of (later famous) portraits of her. *Vecher* (Evening), 1912, her first book, love lyrics, plus her second, *Chetki* (A Rosary), 1914, projecting the attitude of a worldly lover, brought her renown. *Belaya staya* (The White Flock), 1917, and *Anno Domini*, 1922, declared her Russianness, her refusal to emigrate, and her emotional and intellectual independence.

She bore her and Gumilev's son, Lev, in 1912 but left him initially to her parents to bring up. She and Gumilev divorced in 1917; she married very unsuccessfully in 1918; in 1921 Gumilev was executed for alleged counterrevolutionary treason; in 1926 she began living with the art critic Nikolai Punin; in 1928 she divorced Vladimir Shileiko, her actual husband; by 1940 both her lover Punin and her son Lev had been arrested and sent to labor camps. And her work was completely suppressed.

During this period, living on a meager pension, she researched Pushkin; her essays were published posthumously. During the war years, she prepared two long poems which crowned her reputation: *Requiem* and *Poem without a Hero*.

A postwar attack on her and on the short-story writer Zosh-chenko led to her expulsion from the Writer' Union, forcing her to live hand-to-mouth by translating. Not until the rehabilitations of 1957-8 did her son return from prison and her work find publication: *Beg vremeni* (Time's Flight) appeared in 1958. Italy bestowed the Taormina Prize on her in 1964; Oxford University, an honorary degree in 1965. In her last years, as the unofficial dean of Russian poets, she actively supported young people's work, in particular that of Dmitry Bobyshev (her favorite), Anatoly Naiman, Yevgeny Rein, and Iosif Brodsky. Her legacy includes exquisitely crafted, understated, ironic and passionate verse — the fire of love leading to the ashes of grief — a woman's voice expressing a woman's point of view — as well as a powerful cry of the sufferings caused by the years of political repression (*Requiem*) and a complex narrative-in-verse setting autobiographical facts of her life in the context of her country's history (*Poem without a Hero*).

A number of translations of her poetry into English are available, the most thorough being the two-volume, bilingual *The Complete Poems of Anna Akhmatova*, Judith Hemschemeyer, transl., Roberta Reeder, ed., Somerville: Zephyr Press, 1990.

TUESDAY

102 Mikhail Alexeyev: Mikhail Pavlovich Alekseyev (1896-1981) started out wanting to be an opera singer and a poet. He graduated from Kiev University in 1918 and forty years later became a member of the U.S.S.R. Academy of Sciences, serving as chairman of the Division of Russian and Foreign Literary Relations in the Institute of Russian Literature from the mid 1930s until his death. He catalogued Voltaire's library, documented Pushkin's connections with world literature, directed studies of Shakespeare, often represented Russia at international literary conferences, and, by his knowledge, amiability, tact and energy created renewed respect for Russian literature and scholarship throughout the West.

102 what is now Kirov Prospect: These days Kirov Prospect is Seaside Avenue leading on from the Vyborg Embankment.

103 A spirited view of the Frost-Akhmatova meeting is found in the memoirs of Kornei Chukovsky's outspokenly dissident daughter, the novelist and editor Lydia Korneyevna Chukovskaya, author of *Sof'ya Petrovna* (translated as The Deserted House, 1967) and *Spusk pod vodu* (Going Under, 1972). Long a true friend of Akhmatova, she memorialized her in a conversational tone, *Zapiski ob Anne Akhmatovoi* (Paris, 1976) from which the following is taken:

Anna Andreyevna told me about Frost. Apparently he had never heard a thing about her or about her poetry, but Franklin Reeve insisted on their meeting. Naturally there was no way of inviting foreigners to her "phone booth" [as she called her house at Komarovo]; so, the Alexeyevs arranged a luncheon. Frost gave her an inscribed copy of his book. She referred to it rather offhandedly: "Obviously, he knows nature." About the meeting, she said: "We sat in comfortable armchairs facing each other, two old folks. I kept thinking — every time he was accepted somewhere, I was excluded; when he received an award, I was publicly humiliated, but the result's the same — we're both Nobel candidates. That's something to think about."

In response, I told her the silly story of my "non-meeting" with Frost. My English isn't very good, but I like his poems —he not only knows nature but is himself in a way one with it. Frost was at Kornei Ivanovich's [her father's] in Peredelkino. Marina [her sister-in-law] was hostess. I had no responsibilities at all, but I wanted to see Frost. The day before he came, though, our little woodlot was overrun — as close to the house as possible — by plainclothesmen and reporters, and when Frost arrived, accompanied by Reeve, the house was overrun by "translators," for whom there was no need in the first place. I found it so unpleasant that I ran off and hid in my woods burrow from where all I could see were the rear ends of the cars next to the garage and the rear ends of the plainclothesmen among the trees. I sat down to work, delighted not to have to be taking part in the farce. But soon I was half-frozen and shivering; I picked up a thermos and, following my own little path, parting branches as I went, headed back to the house for some hot water. The plainclothesmen were somewhat put out: they hadn't expected anyone to come out of the bushes. Downstairs, the house was empty; Kornei Ivanovich and his guests were upstairs. I safely heated the kettle, made tea, filled my thermos, and went out to the porch when I heard my name called out by a woman rushing down the outside stairs — a face I half recognized, most likely one of the Writers' Union translators. She dashed up to me perfectly pleasantly: "Oh, Lydia Korneyevna, hello! You're not leaving? Don't. I can take you upstairs."

"Thank you," I replied. "You forget that I live here, and I don't need permission to see my father." I turned my back and went off again into the woods.

"She surely was very surprised," said Anna Andreyevna. "She honestly wanted to treat you to Frost. As for your being in your own home, you're wrong. When there are foreigners in a house, its hosts aren't the hosts."*

---

* Both of Frost's visits — to Peredelkino and to Komarovo — are described in detail in the book F. D. Reeve, *Robert Frost in Russia*. Boston:Atlantic-Little,Brown, 1964. The book makes clear that Frost was in Peredelkino on August 31 and in Komarovo on September 4. At the Alexeyev luncheon Akhmatova recited two poems: "The Last Rose:" and also —

> *I won't weep for the loss I have suffered,*
> *But don't let me see here and now*
> *The golden stigma of failure*
> *On a still idealistic brow.*

I assume that the quatrain, like "The Last Rose," is dedicated to Joseph Brodsky. Reeve translated Akhmatova's lines for Frost on the spot.

I asked if she thought that foreigners understood the situation.

"Foreigners are of different kinds," she replied, "we're different among ourselves, and even the times are different. Recently it has sometimes been possible to have conversations without translators. To be sure, not without..." and she looked up at the ceiling.

I confessed that I was both delighted and worried that she had been nominated for the Nobel Prize. Just so the story with Pasternak wouldn't repeat itself.

"I've put it out of mind," Anna Andreyevna answered. "It was in this very room that I explained to Boris that there's no point in getting upset. I read him a list of names — Tolstoy didn't get it, Blok didn't, Selma did — so what? Does it make any difference?"

But that wasn't my point. I asked her if she thought her getting the prize would create a scandal?

"Here, no. But over there, of course, they'll fling dirt. America will fight for Frost. I've already gotten interesting evidence — a relative of mine in Paris, Mitya Gumilev's wife, who doesn't know me at all, has already written about me, and the one thing I know about her is that she's good-for-nothing. When Mitya was called into the service, she made him sign a will leaving everything to her. So now I'm in her hands. Real nice."

Anna Andreyevna then took "The Poem" out of a little suitcase and spread it across a chair....

The Nobel Prize in Literature for 1962 went to John Steinbeck.
105 The poet Anatoly Naiman, one of the group of four close to Akhmatova, resented frequently being mistaken for Brodsky,

just as Akhmatova had resented being thought promiscuous when young, like Blok, and therefore identified Lev Gumilev as "my *only* son." In his memoir, *Rasskazy o Anne Akhmatovoi* (Stories about Anna Akhmatova), Moscow, 1989, Naiman reported Akhmatova's response to meeting Frost: "Both were short-listed for the Nobel prize, and the idea of having them meet seemed to literary leaders and supporters especially apt. Afterwards, Akhmatova recalled the get-together sardonically: 'I can just imagine how others saw us, perfect "gran-daddy and gran-mommy."' (That was how a little kid came up to Chukovsky on the street and asked him, "You a gran-daddy or a gran-mommy?") Professor Reeve, who was present, saw everything very differently and described Akhmatova in high style: 'how grand she was but how sad she seemed to be.' She recited "The Last Rose" for Frost: 'for a few seconds we were silent, still.' Akhmatova reported that Frost asked her what sort of gain could be gotten by making pencils out of Komarovo pines. She rose to the tone of the question and replied equally business-like: 'For cutting a tree in this summer-house area there's a five hundred ruble fine.' (She didn't take to poet Frost for the farmery streak in him, as example citing the poem in which he asserted that the man who has nothing to sell is worst of all. She was making it clear that on that level and in those terms a poet really had no business talking.)"

106 "The Last Rose": Although Akhmatova told Frost that "The Last Rose" was scarcely a week old, she had written it a couple of months before. When it appeared in *Novy mir* the following

January, it bore the epigraph and at that time mysterious initials I.B. "The epigraph...is from a poem by Joseph Brodsky, one of Akhmatova's last protégés... Dmitry Bobyshev, the poet and friend of Akhmatova's in her later years, brought her a bouquet of roses for her birthday [June 11]... She told him all faded but one, which produced a 'miracle,' poems to Bobyshev, Brodsky, Anatoly Naiman and Yevgeny Rein, four prolific young poets whom she admired. This poem is the one dedicated to Brodsky." Viktor Zhirmunsky, *Notes to Stikhotvoreniya i poemy*, Leningrad, 1979, as translated and printed in *The Complete Poems of Anna Akhmatova*, vol. II, p.761.

108 Bushmin: Alexander Sergeyevich Bushmin (1910-1983), a nineteenth-century specialist, was the official director of the Institute of Russian Literature. Stepanov was a bibliographical researcher, and Yury Davydovich Levin was a very able, energetic young scholar following in Mikhail Alexeyev's footsteps.

THURSDAY

120 chargé d'affaires, McSweeney: John Morgan McSweeney (1916-deceased) and his wife Heurica took a fancy to Frost even as they entertained him officially. McSweeney went on to serve as ambassador to Bulgaria in the late 1960s.

120 Valentin Katayev: Valentin Petrovich Katayev (1897-1986) worked as a journalist in Odessa during the civil war, moved to Moscow after it, and continued as a correspondent through the next war. In 1946 he joined the editorial board of *Novy mir*, and in 1955 founded the journal *Yunost*, which he directed until 1962. His earlier works were full of humor and inventiveness, like his 1927 play on the housing crisis, *Squaring the Circle*, or his anti-bureaucratic novel of the same year, *The Embezzlers*. His semi-autobiographical work in 1966-7 mixed fact and dream, altered memory and chronology, creating a new kind of fiction. Uniquely among Russian twentieth-century writers, Katayev maintained his position in the Writers' Union at the same time as he continued to write highly respected, original, innovative work.

Almost all his writings have been translated into English at one time or another: see *The Holy Well*, *The Grass of Oblivion*, and *My Diamond Crown*.

120 Georgii Markov: Georgii Mokeyevich Markov (b.1911) as the text suggests, is remembered as a bureaucrat, not a poet.

FRIDAY

131 Khrushchev and Surkov in discussion: At the tête-à-tête with Khrushchev on the balcony of the Gagra guest house, Surkov later made clear to me, Mr. K gave final authorization for publication of Solzhenitsyn's *One Day in the Life of Ivan Denisovich*, which indeed appeared in the November *Novy mir*.

SATURDAY

145 Demyan Bedny: the pseudonym of Yefim Alekseyevich Pridvorov (1883-1945), popular poet, Party member, satirist and

song writer who was expelled from the Party for a comic opera
Bogatyri (Heroes) that mocked the Russian historical past.

AND AFTER

152 August Hecksher: a founding director of the Twentieth Century Fund, in 1963 he wrote a memo which became instrumental in forming the National Endowments of the Arts and
Humanities.

154 "You give your own version of our trip to Moscow," he said:
This reiterates what Frost had written me in October. Udall
had asked me to vet an article he was preparing for *The New
York Times Magazine*. I turned to Frost for permission, and he
told me to go ahead, adding, "You may give your own version
of our trip to Moscow. I have read a lot of your prefaces and
translations. I know that I can trust your understanding. It is
more than just verbal. We teamed up . . . . Didn't we ride Hell-
bent back from Gagra after toasts to miss our plane?"

We sure did.